Letters from a Nut's Family Tree

TED L. NANCY

SCHOLASTIC INC.

**Dedicated to
Louie Marder**

I sure do miss you, Uncle Louie.

ISBN 978-0-545-48877-8

12 11 10 9 8 7 6 5 4 3 2 1   13 14 15 16 17 18/0

Printed in the U.S.A. 23

First printing, September 2013

The display type was set in King George.
The text type was set in Triplex.
Book design by Charice Silverman
Illustrations by Alan Marder

ACKNOWLEDGEMENTS

A hearty shout-out and solid hello to:

Phyllis Murphy, who makes my life great. And deserves her own line in the Acknowledgments. She was with me when we created Ted L. Nancy.

Dan Strone, who got this book going. Kseniya Zaslavskaya, assistant to Dan Strone. Linda Shaw. Ann & William Hunt. Alyson Daar. Renee Carter. Philip Halpern. Stephan Yarian. Michael Marder. Brent Kimball. Justin Marder—always thinking of you. Hershel Pearl. Johnny Dark. Dr. Mickey Weisberg & Jeanne. Marty & Dee Weisberg. Marilyn & Henri Deutsch. Cele & George Weisberg. Susan Marder. Whitey Marder. Barry Marder. Alan Marder. Marty and Rita Marder. Dr. Gerard and his staff—Mel, Anna, Irma. Eric Bjorgum. Larry Kopeikin. Zack Clark, Charice Silverman, Alan Gottlieb, Alix Inchausti, Jennifer Rinaldi, and the fantastic crew at Scholastic.

Special thanks to Jerry Seinfeld. He makes a difference in my life every day.

Ted L. Nancy's
Family Tree

FUNYUN T. NANCY
1863 – 1955

OLAF Z. NANCYVICH
1510 – 1573

TED L. NANCY XIV
1662 – 1761

THEODORA D. NANCI
1470 – 1561

CELLPHONIAS T. NANCY
1310 BC – 1248 BC

UGH LEE NANCY
428 BC – 306 BC

by

Ted L. Nancy

May I introduce myself to you? My name is Ted L. Nancy. And I write letters.

I've written to businesses, dignitaries, celebrities, corporations, sports teams, average folks, the king of Tonga—just about everybody. I've written with requests, ideas, help with travel, situations I have, problems, concerns, selling ham sandwiches in bathrooms—just about everything. And they answered me!

Some of the letters I wrote include wanting to check into a hotel with my own ice machine. Or telling a department store their mannequin looks like a deceased neighbor and I want to give the mannequin to the family to help with their grieving.

I put those letters and replies in a series of books called LETTERS FROM A NUT. Three of the books were published way before there were emails. Just good old-fashioned letter writing.

To give you an idea, here's a few from that time:

TED L. NANCY
560 N. Moorpark RD. #236
Thousand Oaks, CA 91360

City Offices
City of Greensboro
PO Box 3136
Greensboro, NC 27402   Sept 17, 1996

Dear City Of Greensboro.

I was planning to move to Omaha, Nebraska soon. I wrote to them
and explained that I had heard they were changing the traffic
lights in Omaha to the following:

Red - Go
Green - Stop Suddenly
Yellow - Race Through Light
Plaid - Check Things Out, Then Proceed Accordingly

They wrote me back and said they were not planning on changing the
lights. Red was still stop, green go. they welcomed me to Omaha.
I belched up a fig.

Now I am writing to you, the City of Greensboro, as I have changed
my plans. I will NOT be moving to Omaha shortly. I am moving to
Greensboro shortly. I have heard that you will now change the
traffic lights to the following:

Red - Get Out Of Your Car As It Moves. Honk Horn Furiously. Then
Go
Green - Screech To A Stop. Announce You're Irish. Drift Into
Lane
Yellow - Will Have Happy Face On Light
Plaid - Is Same As Omaha

What is going on there? In California we just see the light and
proceed accordingly according to Roberts Rules Of Traffic

Please let me know this pressing answer as I will be driving into
No. Carolina soon in my car. (I drive a 1983 Le Car. with no
door on passenger side. Bought used at Sarasota clown college)

Sincerely,

Ted L Nancy
Ted L. Nancy.

DEPARTMENT OF TRANSPORTATION
P.O. BOX 3136
GREENSBORO, NC 27402-3136
TELEPHONE: (910) 373-2332
FAX NO: (910) 373-2544

CITY OF GREENSBORO

NORTH CAROLINA

September 24, 1996

Mr. Ted L. Nancy
560 North Moorpark Road
#236
Thousand Oaks, California 91360

Dear Mr. Nancy:

Thank you for your recent letter of inquiry concerning alleged changes to the Greensboro traffic signal system.

Please be assured that traffic signal indications in Greensboro are identical, in meaning as well as color, to those in California with which you are familiar. Additionally, no changes are planned. Nationwide standardization of such signal characteristics is, in fact, mandated by the Federal Highway Administration.

Please feel free to contact me at (910) 373-2860 if you have questions, or if I can be of any other assistance.

Ted L. Nancy
560 N. Moorpark Rd. Suite #236
Thousand Oaks, CA 91360

City Events Planner
CITY OF BUTTE FALLS
431 Broad St.
Butte Falls, OR 97522   Dec 2, 1997

Dear City Of Butte Falls Event Planner,

I am the owner of Henrique's Hens. There are 1,034 hens that do
Civil War reenactments. Some hens fought for the North and some
hens fought for the South. THERE IS NO DANGER TO THE HENS! I
dress them up in little costumes and they charge each other. I
have them trained to also go into a tent and see my Mr. Lincoln
chicken. (mole now stays on)

Last year I presented these same hens in a recreation of the last
days of Disco at Studio 54. (But my Liza Minelli hen pecked a man
named Arthur). NO ONE MISTREATS ANY HENS!

I would like to present this show free for your stressed out and
ragged city employees. Those that need relief and calming down
and want to see a hen battlefield reenactment. You'll speak to a
Leona Dust in my Ogden office. let her wash her hair out in the
snack room sink before you call.

I have heard your city is hospitable towards hen entertainment. i
look forward to my reply, Thanks Butte Falls, truly America's
downtown city. MY HENS ARE WELL CARED FOR!

Sincerely,

Ted L. Nancy
Pres Henrique's Hens

Town of Butte Falls

Altitude Over 2400 Feet
In the Land of Pure Water, Pure Air, Sunshine and Health
Butte Falls, Oregon 97522

December 16, 1997

Ted Nancy
560 No. Moorpark Rd.
Suite #236
Thousand Oaks, CA   91360

Dear Mr. Nancy:

The Mayor and Council Members have to respectfully decline your offer
to put on a hen show. Thank you for thinking so highly of our little
town, we agree with you. Thank you for writing and have a very Merry
Christmas and a Happy New Year.

Sincerely,

City Recorder

MORE HELLO

Now that you see what I do, let me explain to you just what is going on.

I have been working on a brand-new LETTERS FROM A NUT book. Today with emails, there are many opportunities to reach out to new people I know wanted to hear from me. So I started writing new letters in 2009 and sending them out. Now, I am just like you. I watch TV and my favorite show is *Storage Auction Wars*. That's the one where people buy abandoned storage lockers and see what's in there. So I decided to go to a storage auction myself. ROY! Excuse this outburst. I suffer from a problem where I yell out men's names. I cannot control myself. I am currently on Canadian Internet prescription medications and must deal with this affliction. TONY! *Sorreee.*

To continue: Who doesn't want to rummage through other people's junk? Huh? I mean this is stuff they abandoned. I saw my local storage company—Your Stuff Is Piling Up—was holding an auction. I was intrigued, curious, and one other word from the thesaurus. Perhaps I would find a box of varnish-crusted paintbrushes, or some Duran Duran cassettes that I could not play since I do not have a cassette player.

AT THE STORAGE PLACE: I arrived in my car. I drive a Chevy Macaroni, Chevy's sporty new flailabout. I walked to the storage unit area. There were many people there. The auctioneer started with his fast-talking gibberish explaining these were unclaimed units. You could look inside, but not go inside. Then you could bid.

They cut the lock and opened the sliding metal door, and everybody looked inside. The first locker did not interest me at all. All I saw were boxes marked "SPATULAS," "VHS TAPES," "GRANNY'S HEAD"— then, happily, underneath—"FOR HER WIG." I declined. It was a firm decline.

The second locker, the same. When they slid open the metal door, there was a Chinese family living in there. They were eating their lunch. I think it was rice and some sort of broccoli dish. HECTOR! I guessed they lived there. I declined.

However, on the third locker opened—for whatever reason—maybe it's Karma, or luck, or just intuition—I bid. There didn't seem to be anything special about this locker. More boxes, an old mattress, a bicycle, some Pac-Man games from the '80s. And after a frenzy of shouting and yelling, and shouting some more, and amounts being called out, and more yelling, and pushing . . . I ended up with the locker. Unit #23, Your Stuff Is Piling Up, San Miguel, California.

The crowd dispersed and I immediately went to work scrounging through that locker to see what I bought. I opened a box of girls' berets and another box with nothing but bubble wrap, and then I moved an end table only to see another end table. Then I moved the mattress and there was yet another end table. Is there no end to these end tables? Ha-ha-ha-ha-ha. I found somebody's dad's old Members Only jacket. Now, let me just tell you here and now about these Members Only jackets. They were once cool. Today the membership has dwindled to disoriented seniors with pasta stains on their jacket. You can now order the jacket with marinara already on there.

And then there it was.

THE ROCK: What was this odd rock? It seemed to be a stone with some odd markings on it. Like it was from some time very, very long ago. (That's two *verys*. In the *very* world, two is good. Three is the most. To get three *verys* is rare. This rock will be changed to three later when I find out what I truly had.) I pulled the sliding metal door down, put a new lock on Unit #23, yelled out a shrimp dish, and left.

The following shrimp dishes are acceptable to yell out:

Shrimp Scampi
Sweet and Sour Shrimp
Shrimp Andy

AT MY HOME: I looked at the rock with the odd markings on it. Then I went to my computer and Googled "Rock with odd markings on it." A few websites came up for ancient archaeological finds. And twenty-six listings for JCPenney. I have noticed that no matter what you Google, JCPenney comes up. *You want ancient archaeological rocks with odd markings? JCPenney has them on sale.*

I ordered neon bicycle shorts from Penney's and went to an ancient biblical website where I saw the exact same rock with the markings on it. It was from really, really long ago. (That's two *reallys*. In the world of *reallys*, two is very good. There are no three *reallys*.) The ancient rock's page had a link to a website called Your Family Belongs in a Tree Genealogy Services. I clicked on it. That website linked me to a very respected academic. Someone who specialized in tracing one's family tree back. He lived near me.

And that is where this story really, really begins. . . .

CALVIN SOCK: The screen door opened and Dr. Sock greeted me. Now, let me just tell you here and now about Calvin Sock. He kept his eyes closed the entire time and showed me his gums. He had tiny teeth like a pumpkin.

He is a professor at the University of Burma Online. He is highly respected in the Internet-school world. Many of his students have gone on to work out of their homes.

"Let me tell you what I like about earning your degree on the Internet," he told me. "Parking. You're already home. No need to get in your car, drive anywhere, park, get out of your car." Then he smeared cupcake frosting on his face and yelled out a Thai dish. The following Thai dishes are acceptable to yell out:

Pad Thai Noodle
Mee Crob
Massaman Beef Curry

The following Thai dish has been removed from the list:

Satay Gai (Chicken with satay sauce): DO NOT YELL IT OUT!

Calvin Sock examined my old rock with the markings on it. "Do you have any idea just how far your family traces to?"

I did not.

"Let's go back," he said.

At the Beginning of Nothing
The Nancys Are There

Before Time – 1 BC

OCTAVIOUS X. NANCY
80 BC – 11 BC

ARISTOTLE ONANCY
458 BC – 379 BC

UGH LEE NANCY
428 BC – 306 BC

CELLPHONIAS T. NANCY
1310 BC – 1248 BC

EZEKIAS Z. NANCY
6102 BC – 6051 BC

EZEKIAS Z. NANCY: A beard is the only known image of him.

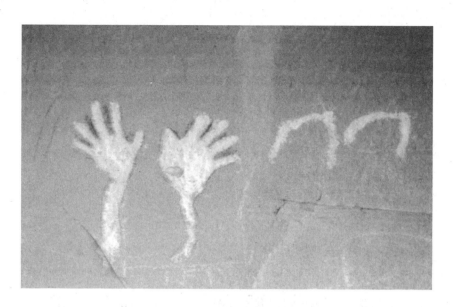

Rock from a Meteor Before the Beginning of Time
Found in Storage Unit #23, Your Stuff Is Piling Up,
San Miguel, California

Translated by Calvin Sock:

"Is anybody out there to write to? Nobody?"

And it was marked:

"Ted L. Nancy"

Apparently Ted L. Nancy is the first name before time or life was formed.

LARRY NANCY
#2 Garden Of Eden Estates
Eden Gardens, Earth

ADAM & EVE
#1 Garden Of Eden Estates
Eden Gardens, Earth   Jan 1, 0001

Dear Adam & Eve,

My name is Larry. I am your neighbor in Apartment #2. Just a
friendly note put through the knot in your tree. I would like to be
respectful here and neighborly, but could you please stop making
noise in your apartment. The crunching of your apple is very
loud and is annoying me. The walls in these units are thin and
your apple crunching keeps me from sitting here doing nothing.

Us being the only 3 people on earth, we can somehow make this
work. If we can't do this at this time with 3 people then we will be
in big trouble in the future when there are more people.

I HAVE NOTHING TO DO! I CAN'T READ ANYMORE! THERE IS
NOTHING LEFT TO LOOK AT! Thank you.

Larry Nancy
Your Neighbor in #2

NOTE: There is no known reply. Scholars unearthed this
of the first 3 people on earth. Adam and Eve and Larry.*

* Also first person to complain about neighbor.

MARK'S ARK CLEANUP

"Pet Problems? No Problem! Lets Us Clean Your Pet Mess"

EZEKIAS Z. NANCY owner
21 Dead Sea Lane
Babylonia, Mesopotamia

INVOICE

TO: NOAH SARKISHIAN
c/o Noah's Ark
Mt. Ararat, Turkey   May 21 6023 BC

Removal 60,000 pounds animal poop from boat. Wash oars (Double charge for 2 animals each)

Sanitize wooden floors. Refresh and deodorize restrooms (flood scent)

Mop rainwater after 40 days & 40 nights

Remove sticks from 1,000 Unicorndogs. Trash.

Also: Spray Wash NOAH'S CART. Replace floor mats, whitewall tires, detail interior, turtle wax w/ 2 turtles.

DUE NOW: 65.00 Shekels

THANK YOU!

PAID

Cellphonias T. Nancy
1 Og Rd #27, Greek Isles, Greece

Moses
#7 Wandering Desert Lane
Mount Nebo, Jordan   1876 BC

Dear Moses,

I am a big fan of yours. I love the Ten Commandments. Any chance
of an 11th? Can you send me an autograph picture? I will show
others. Then i will not show it to them anymore.

Do you have any more miracles you will be doing? Please put me on
your mailing list. The burning bush is great. What else is on tap.?

Respectfully, .
Cellphonias T. Nancy
Cellphonias T. Nancy

TO CELLPHONIAS

Best, Moses

Cellphonias T. Nancy
1 Og Rd Apt #27,
Greek Isles, Greece

HERCULES
Mount Olympus
Crete, Greece   1279 B.C.

Dear Hercules

My name is Cellphonias T. Nancy. I am not a strongman like you. I
am just an ordinary mid sized man. (a medium; Waist 51)

I have a gardening company. I would like you to be our spokesman.
My company is called:

HERCU LEAVES

Our slogan is: "We Have Strongmen Who Blow Leaves Around"

You would go to events for us as our spokesperson. Lion fights,
zeus type stuff, sandal store openings. I can offer you 1200
Darmach. Please let me know by 1278 B.C. As I also have an offer out
to a man named Mitch.   I am enclosing our flyer

Thank you,

Cellphonias T. Nancy
Cellphonias T. Nancy

HERCU LEAVES

"Blowing Leaves Around Is All We Do."

Cellphonias T. Nancy. Prop

HERCU LEAVES

Dear Mr. Nancy,

All business offers should go through my Manager
Please contact:
Hershel Goldman at The Strong Agency.

Thank You,

Hercules
Hercules

ARISTOTLE ONANCY
Zeus Productions
171 Olive St.
Crete, Greece

Bookings Parthenon
#1 Temple Way
Athens, Greece   Feb 27, 420 BC

Dear Parthenon Bookings.

I am putting on the musical "GREECE" and would like to book your Parthenon to stage my production from Aug 1, 420 BC until Nov 15, 420 BC. "GREECE" stars Stavros Travoltaopolis and Olivia Newton Fig.

The Musical is about good girl Sandy and greaser Danny who fall in love. In the summer of 425 BC, local boy Danny Zuko (Stavros Travoltaopolis) and vacationing Sandy Olsson (Olivia Newton Fig) meet at the beach and fall in love. When the summer comes to an end, Sandy, who is going back to Australia, frets that they may never meet again, but Danny tells her that their love is "only the beginning".

We will substitute the Temple Of Apollo for Rydell High School. (could use Acropolis if Apollo not available)

Please write back and let me know how we may proceed. Not even the gods can better this evening.

I look forward to presenting this exciting new musical at your Parthenon Temple. I once saw Rhianna Xenia in "BOY TROY" at the Erechtheion and was delighted. Show will include songs: "Hopelessly Devoted To Plato" & "You're The One I Want. "

Sincerely,

Aristotle Onancy
ARISTOTLE ONANCY
Zeus Productions

The Parthenon
"Greece's Premier Theatre"
Battle Of Delphi Military 1/2 Price

IPTHENIA PAPADOPOULOS
ADMINISTRATION
PARTHENON
ATHENS, GREECE

ARISTOTLE ONANCY
ZEUS PRODUCTIONS
171 OLIVE WAY
CRETE, GREECE   FEB 27, 420 BC

DEAR MR. ONANCY.

LET IT NOT BE! PLEASE BE ADVISED THAT THE PARTHENON IS
CURRENTLY BOOKED DURING THOSE DATES. WE ARE PRESENTING
"SKINBAD THE SAILOR. WARRIOR OF DERMATOLOGY"

AFTER THAT WE ARE REMODELING FOR 100 YEARS. THERE WILL BE NO
APPLE OF DISCORD.

THANK YOU FOR YOUR INTEREST IN THE PARTHENON, "GREECE'S BEST
PLACE TO SEE A SHOW".

RESPECTFULLY,

IPTHENIA PAPADOPOULOS
ASST TO APOLLO, GODDESS OF WISDOM
ADMINISTRATION PARTHENON

UGH LEE NANCY
#1 Yahtzee Way
Yo Yo, China

CONFUCIUS
孔夫子; 221 Takeout Lane
Qufu, Zhou Dynasty, China   Jul 6, 490 BC

Dear Confucius.

I love your "CONFUCIUS SAY" column in our newspaper. Next to WORD
JUMBLES it is my favorite thing. Some of my favorite Confucius
sayings are:

"Man who live in glass house wealthier than man who live in glass
trailer."

"It's not whether you win or lose. Did I say that?   That Wrong."

I belched up a noodle after reading those. Wash my frog. I need
that.

I came up with a few "Confucius Say" sayings. Feel free to use
them in your newspaper column. Just credit me – something like –
Confucius Say Ugh Lee Nancy's Thoughts:

"If you can't say something nice about a person...Find someone
else who can't say something nice about that person and agree with
them."

"Revenge is best served cold. But hot is OK too. As long as you
get revenge."

"No Shirt, No Shoes, No Service. Flip Flops Are Not Shoes. Let's
get that out there."

Let me know what you think, Confucius. I look forward to your
thoughts.

With All The Respect i have For Sayings,

Ugh Lee Nancy

CONFUCIUS
孔夫子; 221 Takeout Lane, Qufu, Zhou Dynasty, China

UGH LEE NANCY
#1 Yahtzee Way, Yo Yo, China   Aug 15, 490 BC

Dear Ugh Lee Nancy

I am so sorry for the long delay in answering you. I was on a journey of a thousand miles that began with the first step. But I had a blister on my foot and stopped for a band-aid. It fell off in Miami.

Thank you for your very nice compliment. I am honored. I have a few more sayings you may enjoy:

"Man who build Great Wall Of China soon faced with huge graffiti problem."

"Fool me once shame on you. Fool me twice shame on me. Fool me three times it is a shame what I am going to do to you."

"Don't forget to tip your waiter." (that's all I got)

You like? Many thank you's.
Confucius
Confucius
(Also working on "Employees Must Wash Hands". But not ready yet; need more)

P.S. I am so tired of coming up with witty sayings. How about just a nice "hello?"

I CAME, I SAW, I CONQUERED PARTY PLANNERS

OCTAVIOUS X. NANCY PROP.
121 SANDINEYE LANE
SPHINX, EGYPT

CLEOPATRA
IMPERIAL PALACE OF EGYPT
21 SANDINSHOE RD.
MACEDONIA, EGYPT   JUNE 2ND, 51 BC

DEAR CLEOPATRA,

THIS PARCHMENT CONFIRMS YOUR ORDER FOR OUR PARTY PACKAGE ON: JULY 25TH, 51 BC. FOR YOU CORONATION AS QUEEN OF EGYPT.

INCLUDES: FOLDING CHAIRS FOR 30,000, PAPER NAPKINS, PLASTIC FORKS, 400 THREAD COUNT EGYPTIAN COTTON CANDY. CONFETTI. REMEMBER, WITH OUR CONFETTI - YOU THROW UP.

I RECENTLY DID AN IDES OF MARCH PARTY FOR PYRAMID RESORTS IN ROME. THEY PARTIED LIKE IT WAS 62 BC. **SANDALS!** EXCUSE THE OUTBURST. I HAVE A PROBLEM. I YELL OUT GLADIATOR REFERENCES WHEN STRESSED. **THUMBS UP!** (SORREE. AM DEALING WITH IT) **CHARIOT!!**

ALSO YOU REQUESTED CLAUDIUS THE CROSS-EYED JUGGLING CHAINSAW CLOWN. HE TRIES MOVING AROUND THE SAND IN ILL FITTING FOOTWEAR WITH CHAINSAWS,

(ON A PERSONAL NOTE, I KNEW YOU AS INEZ FUDD BEFORE YOU WERE CLEOPATRA. TOGA BAR FEB 17, 52 BC. GAVE YOU NUMBER NEVER HEARD FROM YOU.)

I OFTEN REGRET I HAVE SPOKEN. NEVER THAT I HAVE BEEN SILENT.

OCTAVIOUS X. NANCY
OCTAVIOUS X. NANCY

C

CLEOPATRA
Imperial Palace Of Egypt
21 Sandinshoe Rd.
Macedonia, Egypt

OCTAVIOUS X. NANCY
Party Planner
121 Sandineye Lane
Sphinx, Egypt   Aug 17, 51 BC

Dear Mr. Nancy,

This is to advise you that we DID NOT place an order for my Coronation with your company.

This event is being handled by Brutus Party Planners which we have given a deposit to.

In addition we have already booked the Ventriliquist: Wrapping Wray & His Mummy.

I am sorry for this mix-up.
There grows no wheat where there is no grain.

Cleopatra

Cleopatra
(Inez Fudd – Do remember you, Call Me)

23

A Ted L. Nancy
Family Tree Truth

DID JULIUS CAESAR invent the Caesar Salad?

NO! Julius Caesar did not invent the Caesar Salad.

He had lettuce, garlic croutons, grated cheese, anchovies, bacon bits, vinegar & oil dressing but never figured out how to put them together.

They just sat there in front of him for years. He ate them individually but never thought of putting them together in a bowl.

Although he did take credit for the Orange Julius.

I CONTINUE MY JOURNEY

Hello. ~~May I introduce myself to you? I am~~

I wrote that already; I am embarrassed. I drift a bit. *Sorreee!*

I looked through the very old letters you just read. Dr. Sock had linked me, Ted L. Nancy, to the beginning of time. Then to Larry Nancy, who was there at the birth of man, who through the ages had many relatives who birthed more Nancys. My head was dizzy. But not from this. It was just dizzy. But I still had my latest LETTERS FROM A NUT book to work on. The publisher was asking to see the letters I had written and if I got any replies back. I knew I had to really buckle down.

There was a message on my phone. "Mr. Nancy, my name is Magnus Cramp and I live in Scotland. I have some mail here you may be interested in. It's a letter from an ancestor of yours. It's pretty old."

The next day I found myself at the airport. Now, let me just tell you here and now about the airport. It's a giant building where everybody carries all their underwear in their suitcase. Departures are for clean underwear. Arrivals are for dirty underwear.

I went through security and soon I was on Southwest Funjet Flight 17A to Scotland. I settled in for the long nineteen-hour flight. Immediately the person in front of me put his seat down. When the person in front of you puts his seat down, his head becomes your whole flight. *I'm reading now with your head. Now I'm having my dinner with your head. Here, I'll put my drink on your head.*

I landed in Scotland and rented a car. It was a Buick Pimento, Buick's tiny little red car with a weird green thing on top. I only drive Buicks and have told anyone who listens just that. I drove to the tiny village of Dunderclump in the hills of Wee Kirk O' Pippsy. As I drove through the beautiful Scottish countryside, I noticed how serene the land was. Almost like a still painting. After seeing two sightings of the Loch Ness monster jumping out of the lake and letting tourists snap pictures of it, I arrived at a small cottage. And that is where I met . . .

MAGNUS CRAMP: No finer Scotsman will you find. At least that's what he told me. He was big, with a round face and a stupid haircut. He liked to pose from the side.

He welcomed me into his house. It was a small, comfortable home with many pictures of Taylor Lautner around. "I like Taylor Lautner," he explained. "But I think my favorite actor now is Mila Kunis. She was great in that swan movie. And I don't like swans. They flap way too much—"

I cut him off. I realized he was meandering and made little sense. But who was I to judge? After a snack of haggis, kippers, lamb pie, lucky tatties, more haggis, and Dundee marmalade, we settled in. (Mind you, this was just a snack.)

"Mr. Nancy, I have enjoyed your books for years," he told me. "I am an avid reader and all I read are old MapQuest directions and your letter books. That is why what I am about to show you should interest you, my friend." He offered me a plate of Clootie dumplings and some more haggis. I declined. It was a semifirm decline.

Magnus Cramp pulled out a large envelope from under his couch, then fell forward from his weight. He looked at the document inside for a moment, then handed it to me.

It was a letter, and my eyes immediately went to the date. October 3, 1127. "Is that 1127, like nine hundred years ago?" I asked.

"Yes," he said. "It appears to be from a relative of yours, a Sir Nancy the Brave." He sucked on a hard candy. It was lemon and he really sucked it down to a sliver, making those sucking noises that are annoying. Getting every bit of flavor out of that lemon candy. I belched up a kipper and yelled out the name McGinty. He did not respond.

"It looks like it's some sort of request to open a business in medieval times," I answered.

"And there's a reply." Then he drifted again. "Forget Taylor Lautner and Mila Kunis. I like the music of Nicki Minaj. She—"

I cut him off. I needed to focus. On. Me.

And so, with my visit to Magnus Cramp, he of the tiny village of Dunderclump in the hills of Wee Kirk O' Pippsy, I continued my family-tree journey, tracing my lineage. . . .

Middle Ages

We Have a Baboon in Our Family

1100 – 1600

OLAF Z. NANCYVICH
1510 – 1573

BENVOLIO MONTAGUE NANCY
1550 –1623

SIR NANCY THE BRAVE
1101 – 1192

THEODORA D. NANCI
1470 – 1561

OLAF Z. NANCYVICH: The son of Theodora D. Nanci. Theodora adopted a baboon who many believe was a Bigfoot. He was smarter than her real son, Mitchell. When the town realized Theodora had adopted a baboon, she had to return all the gifts from the baby shower. (Including plush toys.)

Sir Nancy The Brave
17 Penny Face Rd, The Forest of Coucy

Business Licenses & Applications
CITY OF CAMELOT
38300 Yorkshire Bridge, Camelot, England   Oct 3, 1127

Dear City Of Camelot Business Licenses,

My good day, fine people. I throw the gauntlet down. I inquire about what happened to my application i sent you a six-month ago. This is for my Comedy Club: SIR LAFFS A LOT. (Formerly JOUSTERS)

Sir Laffs A Lot is a 22 Round Table comedy club in The Chateau Galliard Castle in Camelot opening soon. Our Bill Of Faire will be: beef, fowl, goose puffs, cheese partridges, chalupas, & our signature 72 ounce Merlin Slurpee. There is a 2 goblet minimum. Must be in window: YES WE HAVE DRAGON MELTS!

My check has been cashed by your office. Papers were filled out by our manager Anne of Cleves. Our Ventriloquist: Minstrel Morry and His Fool is our opening court jester. His act: MY PUPPET WILL NOT SHUT UP AND IS DRIVING ME CRAZY has been booked for a fortnight. I have over 2,000 t-shirts waiting for my application approval. I was told to write you with this information when I sent a pigeon to your office . Moat parking permits, please. Thank you for your assistance.
Respectfully,
Sir Nancy The Brave
NO SHIRT, NO SHOES, NO ARMOR, NO SERVICE

CITY OF CAMELOT
GATEWAY TO SHERWOOD FOREST
"Come for The Grog - Stay For The Damsels!"

Hear Ye! Hear Ye!

Sarah 14th Kings Council
Administration
CITY OF CAMELOT
38300 Yorkshire Bridge
Camelot, England

Sir Nancy The Brave
17 Penny Pie Rd
The Forest of Coucy   Oct 23, 1127

Dear Squire Nancy -

PROCLAMATION: By order of his Majesty King Arthur Lord Of
Camelot and 11 adjoining regions we declare:

> We have received **NO** application for your comedy
> Club **SIR LAFFS A LOT**

IN ADDITION: We already have a business in that space in Gulliard castle:

HOUSE OF LORDS ARMOR SHARPENING AND SHOE REPAIR

There must be confusion, sir.

Order is complete. This 23 day October Year of 1127.

Sarah 14th Kings Council
Administration
CITY OF CAMELOT

Theodora Da Nanci
6 Cobblestone Way
Florence, Italy 023

Sept 4, 1502

LEONARDO DA VINCI
DaVinci Greeting Cards
27 Renaissance Blvd.
Florence, Italy 121

Dear Artist Leonardo Da Vinci:

Saluto. I know you sell greeting cards with paintings on them.
I've seen your work in gift shops. Magnifico!

Could you do a special request?

I have two dogs — Mona and Lisa. Can you put them on a greeting
card for me?

I'd like to send them out as a Holiday card. I know only a few of
my relatives will see it...But maybe you can do something with
this.

Grazie for your reply.

Please find enclosed a picture of my 2 dogs.

Sincerely,

Theodora Da Nanci

My Dogs

LEONARDO DA VINCI
27 Renaissance Blvd.
Florence, Italy 121

Theodora Da Nanci
6 Cobblestone Way
Florence, Italy 023   Sept 21, 1502

Dear Signora Da Nanci:

I'll make this short and brief.

I am not interested in the faces of your dogs. They hold no
interest for me as an artist.

I am disgusto that you think this has any value to me.

Do not wasto my time anymore!

vi Leonardo de Zina

Signore Leonardo Da Vinci

Theodora Da Nanci
6 Cobblestone Way
Florence, Italy 023

Tickets
DISTINGUISHED SPEAKERS SERIES
Colosseum Box Office
PO BOX 2
Rome, Italy   Jan 4, 1504

Buon Giorno Distinguished Speakers Series,

Scusi. I want 2 tickets for CHRISTOPHER COLUMBUS in your
Distinguished Speakers Series at the Colosseum. Feb 1, 1504.
Loge section please.

I understand Signore Columbus will be talking about his 4 SHIPS —
The Nina, Pinta, Santa Maria, and The Italian Sub. That's the
ship packed with salami, bologna, provolone cheese, pickles,
peppers, oil and vinegar. My friend, Salvatorio, saw him at the
Milan show last year. Lots of laffs.

Will you have parking for my hog? I have a handicapped placard.
(Foot swollen from shopping cart run over incident. Hog, not me)

Will Columbus mention his WORLD IS ROUND routine.? My neighbor,
Beth, saw this in Naples last month and thought it was the
funniest routine she has ever heard. When he got into his "world
is flat Queen Isabella is a moron" rant — Beth almost plotzed.
(Taken from theater in an oxygen tent. Hog, not her)

Please confirm: 8 Tickets Loge Section, Feb 1, 1504, Platinum Hog
Parking.

Arrivederci

Theodora Da Nanci

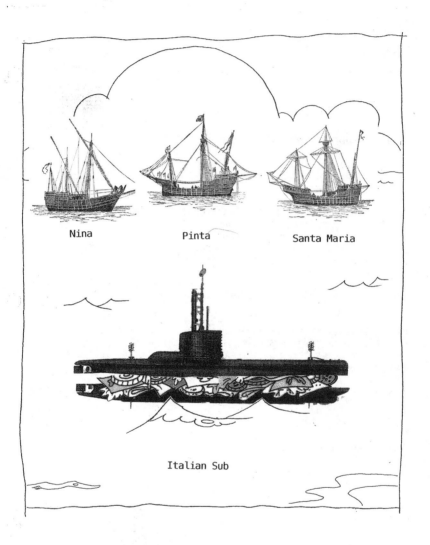

Nina   Pinta   Santa Maria

Italian Sub

THE COLISEUM - "Rome's Place To See And Be Seen"
Disabled Invasion Of Italy Soldiers 1/2 Price

CUSTOMER SERVICE/TICKETS
DISTINGUISHED SPEAKERS SERIES
Colosseum Box Office
PO BOX 2 Rome, Italy

Signora Theodora Da Nanci
6 Cobblestone Way Florence, Italy 023   Jan 17, 1504

Dear Signora Theodora Da Nanci,

Regarding your request to purchase tickets for Christopher Columbus, Distinguished Speakers series for Feb 1, 1504: We are sorry to report that event has been canceled. Signore Columbus has taken ill with the Bubonic Plague.

However, we do offer MICKEY GILLEY on that date as a replacement. Mr. Gilley plays his banjo, mandolin, & flute while a fat lady eats 15 pounds of spaghetti.

If you care to order tickets for this performance we can assist you. We can also offer you Platinum Parking Privileges for your hog if you order by the 30th of Gennaio.

Ciao,

Marcella Lunzi
Tickets

ONE NIGHT ONLY!   1 Feb 1504   SPECIAL EVENTE   COLISEUM ROMA

Signore MICKEY GILLEY   In Person

Plays Banjo. Mandolin. Flute   While a FAT LADY EATS SPAGHETTI*

Here's What The Critics Say:

"As good as entertainment gets" - Guiseppe Floongi. Panini News

"I enjoyed it" - Sam Rubin. Renaissance Times

Coming next week: CARROT CAKE the Prop Court Jester

*NO MEATBALLS THIS PERFORMANCE

Olaf Z. Nancyvich
121 Borscht Blvd
Perm, Russia

Nostradamus
18 Seer St.
Salon-de-Provence, France   MARCH 8, 1557

Dear Nostradamus,

Gormshmim! That is my word for "Greetings" in Russian.

I have been following your predictions since your book was published in 1555.
impressive. I believe some of them will come true one day. Particularly the one
where you predict: "In the year 2012 women will have as many tattoos as men."

Another Nostradamus prediction I believe we will see one day is: "Sneakers will cost
$100.00 a pair."

I am too a prophet. I predict future events. Here are some of my predictions for the
future:

"The can opener will be the biggest invention ever." (as soon as somebody invents
the can)

"In the future we will be able to see moving images through a square box. The
images will change. I will call it a window."

I run the local Olaf Garden Restaurant here. It is a chain restaurant . Our slogan is:
"All the breadsticks you can eat with unlimited salad. Fill up on that so the main
course doesn't look so small."

Let me know...anything.   To the future....Gormsminsk

OLAF

Olaf Nancyvich

Michel de Nostradamus
18 Seer St.Salon-de-Provence, France

Olaf Nancyvich
21 Borscht Blvd
Perm, Russia

Apr 16, 1557

Dear Mr. Olaf Nancyvich,

Bonjmeemi. That is my word for "Greeting." And merci for telling me how much you like my predictions. You may also like my new book: "INSULTS FOR ANY OCCASION" due out in 1558 from Bantam. There are over 1,000 insults in there you can use for any occasion although I don't know how many occasions you will have to insult the same person over and over again.

I enjoyed your predictions very much. They are quite deep and prophetic. You are obviously a thinker and very oracular. We have the same gift. Please, if you will, Olaf, study my latest new predictions for our future. I will put them in quatrains soon.

"People rummaging through Storage Lockers will be the greatest entertainment for the masses. 2nd only to weighing heavy people."

"In 1982 a package of Goobers at the movie theater will cost $6.00 an ounce while silver is $4.00 an ounce. Goobers will cost more than silver"

"Starting with the year 1992 the same rubber gloves will be used to make fast food sandwiches and do brain surgery."

"In the future...Silly names like Google, Yahoo, Tweet, Yelp, & Hotmail" will be the giants of the world replacing U.S. Steel, & World Bank. Ireland will change it's name to Toodly Do."

Au Revoir, fellow seer

Michel de Nostradamus (Terry)

MR. BENVOLIO MONTAGUE NANCY
2704 Kingsbury Rd.
Manchester, England

MR. WILLIAM SHAKESPEARE
86 Drystraw Ave. #16
Stratford-Upon-Avon, England   3 Feb 1590

My Good Dear and Kind Mr. William Shakespeare -

I once knew a Ric Drip who wrote under your name. Is this you? I must confess, sire, I LOVE YOUR WORK! My favorite play of yours is RICHARD III. A most wonderful night at the theater for myself and M'lady. (who may be a zebra) However I did not care for Richard's 1 or 2. LIPSTAIN! Excuse me I blurt out women's cosmetics when excited about good writing. ROUGE BLUSH! Sorreee.

Now. Back to. Me.

I too am a playwright. Amateur at best, but i do write a bit. Could you read my play and give me advice? It is called:

"ROMEO AND JULIET AND LARRY"

It is the story of 2 star crossed lovers - Romeo & Juliet - and their annoying neighbor Larry who keeps sending them notes telling them to "keep it down over there." Eventually the apartment association is called and there are icy stares. PENCILED IN EYEBROWS!!! (Once again an apology for my medical outburst)

I'm also working on "THE REAL MERRY HOUSEWIVES OF WINDSOR". Thank you for your advice.

Respect for your work,

Benvolio Montague Nancy

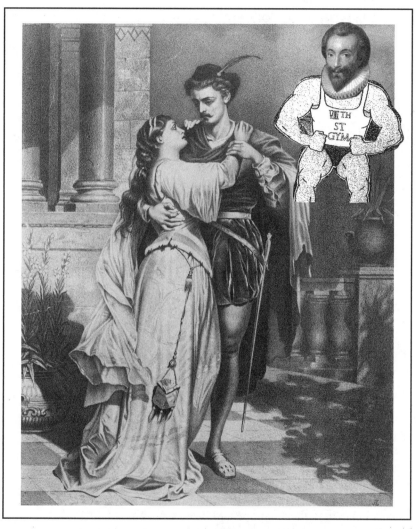

"ROMEO & JULIET & LARRY"

MR. WILLIAM SHAKESPEARE
86 Drystraw Ave. #16
Stratford-Upon-Avon, England

MR. BENVOLIO MONTAGUE NANCY
2704 Kingsbury Rd.
Manchester, England   10 March 1590

My Dearest Mr. Benvolio Montague Nancy:

A fine day to you, kind sir. And thank you
For writing me with your idea for a
Play called "ROMEO & JULIET
& LARRY."

Truthfully I see nothing of value
In this idea, or these characters,
Or the name of the people, or lovers,
Or anything to do with this at all.
There is nothing here for me to grasp my
spirit around.

I am not sure the public would warm to
This subject. I do, however, like Larry
The annoying neighbor.

The character of Romeo has no substance.
I hate the name! However, in new thought,
If Larry would call out to Juliet
With his complaints – she on the balcony –
That may be something an audience would like.
I can see the fair Juliet saying:
"O Larry, Larry! Wherefore art thou Larry?
I am sorry about the juicer noise."

And forget "THE REAL MERRY HOUSEWIVES
OF WINDSOR." Who would watch a show about
Real housewives with heavy rouge stain makeup
On and botched plastic surgery and their problems?
Hope this helps. Keep up the good work.

I am yours in theater.... William Shakespeare

BACK HOME

The letters and replies I just read made me stagger around my living room. I think it was staggering and I think it was my living room. It may not have even been me. I just know somebody was wobbling around somewhere. I put a washcloth on my head and drifted. . . . I think it was a washcloth. . . .

I am the great-great-great-great-(a few more *great*s)-grandson of Benvolio Montague Nancy. My relative actually communicated with William Shakespeare. And gave him the idea for *Romeo and Juliet* (or at least Larry). That is so weird. Me being a writer and all. Here I am, descended from a long line of family letter writers.

I sat on my couch and thought about that. Doritos spilled off my T-shirt. My descendants were involved with Moses and Cleopatra. And Leonardo da Vinci. I had the gene. I was from a long line of nuts. Who knows what this crazy world brings? Huh? Like the girl in my building, in Apartment #22, Loretta Float. Well . . . you know what they say about hitting the lottery. It's as rare as getting hit by lightning. Yesterday, Loretta Float went out to buy a lottery ticket. She bought it from a convenience store—a Stop and Rob. She left the store. And got hit by lightning. SHE SCORED TWICE! What are the odds of that? It wasn't even raining.

As I sat in my apartment thinking about the journey I had just taken to Scotland and all the haggis I had filled up on . . . the phone rang. It was the publisher, Mary Anne Numb, bugging me to see what letters I had for the new LETTERS FROM A NUT book. We were under a deadline to finish that book. So I showed her the new letters I had written and the replies I had received:

1413 1/2 Kenneth Rd. #193
Glendale, CA 91201

Business Licenses
CITY OF ARCADIA
240 West Huntington Dr.
P.O. Box 60021
Arcadia, CA 91066   January 3, 2010

Dear City Of Arcadia,

I am looking to see what happened to my license application for my
comedy club: SOMETHING SMELLS FUNNY

I sent in the paperwork and 75 cents.   I have not heard anything.
SOMETHING SMELLS FUNNY is a 15 seat comedy club in Arcadia
opening soon.   It is modeled after the sewage problem of Medieval
England.

No outside cushions allowed.

My check has been cashed.   Papers were filled out by our manager
Annie Cleave.

Mop Breath & Sir Arthur is our opening headliner Ventriloquist .
Mop Breath wears a suit of armor and jousts with his puppet.   Then
they both sniff the air as I release a "funk" scent reminiscent of
an unsupervised septic system.   You'll think you're back in the
days of Merry Old England.

PLEASE!!   Do Not bring outside Soy Packets in .

Many today are aware of the sewage problem left over from England
in the year 1127.

Thank you for your assistance.   I look forward to my reply.
Please call me F.D.   I like that.

Respectfully,

J. D. Ted L. Nancy

F.D. Ted Nancy

City of
Arcadia

**Development
Services
Department**

January 18, 2010

F.D. Nancy
1413 ½ Kenneth Rd., #193
Glendale, CA 91201

SUBJECT: License

Dear Mr. Nancy:

I have received your letter inquiring about the status of your   license
application for your comedy club (Something Smells Funny); which is to
open in the City of Arcadia.

Please be aware that this office has not received an application with the
above information.

If you have any questions, please feel free to contact me at (626) 574-
5430.

Sincerely,

Business License Officer

*↙ Coffee
mug
stain*

*→ More Coffee
(drip)*

TED L. NANCY
1413 1/2 Kenneth Rd. #193
Glendale, CA 91201

President Ólafur Ragnar Grímsson
Office of the President of Iceland
Sóleyjargata 1
IS-150 Reykjavík, Iceland   6/1/2009

Dear Mr. President of Iceland Ólafur Ragnar Grímsson.

Just a note to say you are the best President of a country
involving ice I have ever seen. HECTOR! I admire and respect
what you have done for Ice People. So do ALL members of our mens
group. Without ice where would we be? Huh? We would have no
cold drinks. and nothing to chew on after the cold drink. No
Swansons frozen TV dinners, no Ice Machines in hotels. (Party!!!)
No names for Rappers like Ice Cube and Ice Tray and Ice Capades.
Call me Antonio when we first meet. I need that. Imagine a whole
nation without ice. Wow! (i can't)

One of our club members remembers you as a professor at the
University of Iceland, He currently drives a septic truck and has
his hair glued down. If you like you could be president of our
air conditioner club. Consider it. Post will be open until
7/12/09. Then Aoalbjörn Gudmunsson will probably get it or maybe
Bjarnhéoinn Vigfusson. They will wrestle for it. Cuff my hem.

Can you please send us an autographed picture we could put on our
refrigerator? So every time we open the freezer door & get a
blast of cold air we are reminded of you.

Keep up the good work.

With utter respect,

Ted L. Nancy
Icelander

OFFICE OF THE
PRESIDENT OF ICELAND

With the compliments
of the office of
The President of Iceland

Staðastaður, Sóleyjargata 1
150 Reykjavík • Iceland
Tel.: 540 4400 • Fax: 562 4802
E-mail: forseti@forseti.is

1.2.2011

Address: Staðastaður, Sóleyjargata 1, IS-150 Reykjavík, Iceland
Tel: +354 540 4400 • Fax: +354 562 4802 • E-mail: president@president.is • www.president.is

I'M OUT AGAIN

I enjoy writing letters and it's nice when my books are used for more than to straighten a wobbly table. Recently I got a letter from a prison warden who told me he used my book *Extra Nutty* to calm prisoners when they rioted. He said my book saved thirty-one mattresses from being burned.

My phone rang. I answered it.

"Mr. Nancy?"

"Yes?"

"Is this Ted L. Nancy?"

"It is. Can I help you?"

And the next thing I knew I was at the airport again. I like that they have luggage shops at the airport. Who forgets this? You're home packing, *Let's see, I have my socks and my underwear and deodorants—I'll just scoop this stuff up in my hands and get on the plane.*

I went through Security again. After accidentally taking someone else's shoes and walking away with their suitcase, I got on the plane. I was very tired. I quickly fell asleep. I slept like a baby. I gummed a teething ring and messed my Rumpsters.

After a twenty-seven-hour flight, I landed in Germany. I now travel with my own overhead bin, so I removed it from the fuselage and exited the craft. Since I also travel with my own skycap and airport curbside loading, my luggage was quick to retrieve. I threw a paper cup on another passenger and walked to the car-rental place.

AT THE CAR-RENTAL COUNTER: I rented a Dodge Fudgesicle. I only drive Dodges. To me they are the finest cars on the road. This one was their sporty new Liftback. Break down, get a lift back. Ha-ha-ha-ha-ha. I yelled out an Indian take-out order and drove off. The following Indian take-out orders are acceptable to yell out:

Tandoori Curry
Mushroom Bhaji
Crabs Bombay

The following dish is no longer available to yell out:

Kalmi Kebab: DO NOT YELL IT OUT!

The countryside of Germany is quite impressive. It is quiet and serene. There was hardly any movement. Except for the UFO that landed and the alien who got out and changed the tire on a tourist's car and took a picture. Other than that, the ride was uneventful to Brachenwurst, a small village in the Bavarian countryside.

I got back to my motel room late in the day. I always stay at Motel 5. It's a step down from Motel 6, but what are numbers anyway? I asked the clerk when I checked in, "What kind of a view do you get for sixty-five dollars a night?"

And he said, "For sixty-five dollars a night, you get a view of someone paying eighty-five dollars a night." He handed me my room key.

I opened the door to Room #2301. The place was grimy. Two cockroaches were playing air guitar. The phone rang.

HORST PRETZEL is a German man, late forties. He greeted me at the door with a tin-foil hat on, goggles, and his fingers in his ears.

"Do you hear popcorn popping? It is very loud," he asked me.

"No," I said. For I did not hear anything.

He invited me into his home. He kept his fingers in his ears.

"Do you hear a carnival passing by?"

"No." I heard nothing.

"Ted, let me show you what I told you about on the phone."

He showed me a letter written on some parchment. "It appears to be from your relative in the year 1651."

I studied the letter, which was certainly written in the way I do, and the man, a Ted El Nancy, had the same name as myself only *El* instead of an *L.* for a middle name. He was Spanish.

"Do you hear someone walking on crunched-up glass?"

"No," I said. For I did not.

"I have more to show you, Ted."

Horst Pretzel then proceeded to show me a knapsack of old letters. I was amazed as I stared at it. They were hundreds of years old.

"These were left to me by my sister who ran off and joined an insane asylum. Do you hear a loud parade? I may even be related to you, Mr. Nancy."

And so—armed with a new knapsack of correspond⸀ relatives—I journeyed on. . . .

Renaissance

My Relative Almost Invents the Sandwich

1601 – 1800

HENRY HAMBURGER NANCY
1732 – 1821

TED L. NANCY XIV
1662 – 1761

TED EL NANCY
1629 – 1699

TED L. NANCY XIV: The only known image of him is his shoe.
People claimed they never saw him. Just his shoe. Apparently
he led a full life as this shoe. Except for a weird toe.

TED EL NANCY
25001 Pinata Place, Barcelona, Spain

Business Licenses
CITY OF SEVILLE
Town Circle Mall, Seville, Spain   SEP 23, 1651

Dear City Of Seville Business Licenses,

Hola, Amigos and Amigas. I am inquiring about the status of my
application i sent you for my Comedy Club: THE PHUNNY PLAGUE

The Phunny Plague is a 78 seat comedy club in La Maestranza Bullring in
Seville that is under construction now. We will have sweet oranges,
roasted hens, corinder seed, stewed ram, & our signature 72 ounce Well
Water Gulp. There is a 2 rat minimum. Must be in window:
YES WE HAVE HUEVOS!

My check has been cashed by your office. Papers were filled out by our
manager Diego De La Peep.

Our headliner is: The Marquis of Figueroa and his Spanish Rice. The
Marquis tells jokes, throws Spanish rice in the air, tells more jokes,
throws more Spanish rice, eats a shrimp, does an impression of King
Fernando III, gets tangled in linen. I have over 2,000 party mugs
waiting for my application approval.

Disease parking permits, please. Thank you for your assistance.

Respectfully,

Ted El Nancy
Owner The Phunny Plague
"Where You Can Laff About The Plague"

CITY OF SEVILLE

"Visit Barber Row!"

Business Licenses
CITY OF SEVILLE
Town Circle Mall
Seville, Spain

SENOR TED EL NANCY
25001 Pinata Place
Barcelona, Spain

Oct 21, 1651

RE: PHUNNY PLAGUE COMEDY CLUB

Dear Senor Ted El Nancy:

Please be advised we have received NO application for your comedy
club opening in Seville.

In addition, you must also get a food permit if your Act is using
Spanish Rice cooked or uncooked. Food, particularly Spanish Rice,
is considered a vessel to carry disease.

The recent Bubonic Plague has caused all considerable anguish and
your entertainment is a concern.

Please re-send your application and have The Marquis Of Figueroa
substitute another dish for rice. Perhaps ceviche.

Guadeloupe Maria Carminita de La Lopedo
Administration
CITY OF SEVILLE

Reservations
PALACE OF VERSAILLES
1 French Fry Blvd, Versailles, France   Aug 10. 1684

Dear Palace Of Versailles Reservations.

Bonjour Innkeeper! A glorious August to you, my front desk
greffier. I will be arriving by pelt and need a room for 3 nights
Sep 1-3, 1684 . Executive accommodations please. I am a traveler.
You have been highly recommended by Le Shower Cap Association of
Orlando.

Now. Down to. My situation.

I travel with my own horrid dungeon in which I keep my decrepit
brother in law Georges XXL hanging on the wall. Please have the
maid AVOID CLEANING THIS ROOM DURING MY STAY. She can
just leave towels and shampoo by the dungeon door.

Rate, please, for the 3 nights and if there is an extra person charge
for the decaying Georges rotting on the wall. Merci beaucoup. Your
hotel is splendid. I once belched up a croissant at your breakfast
buffet. Sep 1-3, 1684. Travelers rate. I am a platinum gold
member with zinc privileges. I will also need an ironing board. is
that invented yet ?
Respect,
Ted L. Nancy The 14th

MS. Fleurie de Lorrain
PALACE OF VERSAILLES
Aide de Camp,
His Majesty Louis XIV
1 French Fry Blvd, Versailles, France

TED L. NANCY XIV
16 Avenue Du Ru Apt 301B, Nice, France   Aug 29, 1684

Bon Jour Monsieur Nancy XIV,

We wish to inform you that the Palace Of Versailles is NOT a hotel. It is a castle and the residence of LOUIS XIV, the King Of France. He lives there with his family and dog Le Andy.

Therefore we cannot offer you accommodations.

We suggest you try the Le Quinta Inn which is 2 blocks from the Palace. They may be able to assist you.

 I understand they are also pet friendly. For your pelt.

Sincerely,

MS. Fleurie de Lorrain
Palace Of Versailles Aide de Camp,
His Majesty Louis XIV

TED L. NANCY THE 14TH
16 Avenue Du Ru Apt 301B
Nice, France

BLACKBEARD THE PIRATE
Latitude 1 Longitude 20
ATLANTIC OCEAN   Dec 3, 1690

AHoy Matey, Blackbeard The Pirate .

Glug glug glug. I'm under water. (just kidding.) I have an inner tube on.
I hope this gets to you in the middle of the Ocean. I paid extra for delivery
to you. (by seagull; name is Andy)

My uncle is a pirate. he never goes to sea. His name is BLACKBOARD
THE PIRATE. he just writes on a blackboard and diagrams what he would
do IF - and that's a big IF - if he went on a pirate ship out to sea. For now
there's just a lot of X's and O's in chalk. I found a doubloon yesterday and
bought a Jolly Roger candy. It was watermelon. Yesterday my neighbor
Ricardo drank a gallon of Clam Steam stood up and yelled out: BLACKEN
MY TUNA! Then collapsed. Went down like a one legged sailor slipping
on a freshly mopped deck.

I once knew a BLACK SOCKS AND SANDALS THE FASHION MISHAP
PIRATE. Glug glug.

Hey! you ever heard of a product called JUST FOR BLACK BEARDS -
TOUCH OF GRAY? It works. Lets you keep a lot of your black beard but
still put some gray in it.

You think they'll ever be a pirate named Jean Lefitte and they'll call him
Stinky? Stinky Le Feet? Ha ha ha Ho Ho Ho Hee Hee Hee.

Send me a picture so i can look at your beard.

Your friend.
Ted L. Nancy XIV

Blackbeard the Pirate.

B.Cole sculp.

THE EARL OF SIDE DISH
HENRY HAMBURGER NANCY
22 Pastrami Rd., Merryville, England

EARL OF SANDWICH
27 Relish Way, Worcester, England   19 December, 1771

My Dearest Earl Of Sandwich.

I once knew a Ron Pancake. Is that you? Please permit me to introduce myself. I am Henry Hamburger Nancy.

However my Royal title is: THE EARL OF SIDE DISH.

I would like to offer my services to assist with your sandwich. I can supply coleslaw or potato salad.

Hey! Do you know THE SQUIRREL OF SANDWICH. He feeds squirrels in the park with pieces of sandwiches. it is a sound business i offer you. There is money to be made. SALAMI! I am sorry but I suffer from an affliction where i yell out random foods. LETTUCE! Please forgive me but I cannot control myself. I am on medication. ONION! I wish there was something I could do. MUSTARD! But I can't. BREAD! I am so sorry. Let us forge a business relation good for all of England.

The Earl Of Sandwich and the Earl Of Side Dish come together to have a complete meal. Yes? No?

I can be reached at the address above.
Good day hungry sir,

HENRY HAMBURGER NANCY
THE EARL OF SIDE DISH

HIS HIGHNESS THE EARL OF SANDWICH

"One bite we gotcha"

The Right Honoble Edward Lord Mountague Viscount Hinchingbrooke Barron of S. Neots Earle of Sandwich

THE EARL OF SOUP OR SALAD
Aid to: THE EARL OF SANDWICH
27 Relish Way, Worcester, England

Sir HENRY HAMBURGER NANCY
Earl Of Side Dish
22 Pastrami Rd. Merryville, England

13 January, 1772

Dear Sir Hamburger Nancy,

I am Aide de Camp to the Earl Of Sandwich. Permit me to introduce myself to you: I am THE EARL OF SOUP OR SALAD

To inform you, sir: we are experimenting: To take the same foods you eat for dinner - steak, potatoes, vegetables - take a smaller portion of the same steak, potatoes, vegetables - wet it - and serve it before you eat your dinner. We call it Soup.

In addition, we have had ongoing discussions with THE EARL OF ONION RINGS OR FRENCH FRIES. We are also working on: THE EARL OF SLIDERS which are mini Earls. .

Thank you for writing us. We remain....

Hungry

The Earl of Soup or Salad

THE EARL OF SOUP OR SALAD
Aide de camp to
THE EARL OF SANDWICH

HENRY HAMBURGER NANCY
22 Pastrami Rd., Merryville, England

BEN FRANKLIN
12 Betsy Ross Way
Philadelphia, PA

Sep 5, 1776

My Dear Good Ben Franklin,

A whistle & a cheerio to you kind man. I have been reading about your accomplishments: Founding Father of the United States, author, Postmaster General, inventor of Mr. Potato Head. Plus your work with electricity is simply marvelous. Bravo!

I would like to order some items from your store:

Ben Franklin Bath Mat
Ben Franklin Soap Caddy
Ben Franklin Mentos Geyser Tube - Sprays candy 25 feet in the air
    (I hope in future you sell this - was told that)

Are the Finger Puppet's in yet?

I do think it's noble a Statesman as yourself with your many distinguishments lends your face and name to shower items. Outstandingly elegant.   Hear Ye! Hear Ye!

I look forward to my purchases.

With Full Respect For The Kite,

Henry Hamburger Nancy

BENJAMIN FRANKLIN

12 Betsy Ross Way, Philadelphia, PA

HENRY HAMBURGER NANCY

22 Pastrami Rd., Merryville, England   Sep 21, 1776

Dearest Mr. Hamburger Nancy:

This is to inform you I DO NOT carry bath items for sale with my face
and name. Furthermore, I find insulting you would suggest I would lend
my good name, which I have spent years building up with the American
People, to personal grooming items. I am insulted, dismayed, and one more
word from my newly printed Thesaurus. In addition, I can not take credit
for Mr. Potato Head That is countryman Thomas Jefferson's creation.
Along with Flute Hero. (I invented Mr. Potato BODY)

I doubt you will ever see my respected name associated with bath products
or something as...as...(looking for word here for disgusting in Thesaurus) as
nonsensical as a 25 foot Mentos Geyser. I am insulted my good man!
Cheerio to you.   Yes, we have the Finger Puppets

Benjamin Franklin

Henry Hamburger Nancy
22 Pastrami Rd.
Merryville, England

PRESIDENT GEORGE WASHINGTON
3 Cherry Street
New York, City, NY   May 23, 1789

Dear President George Washington,

My monkey looks exactly like you. Right down to the teethy smile and weird eyes. The resemblance is uncanny.

His name is Victor. And people always say to me "Your monkey Victor looks just like our new First President." I do see the resemblance.

Please send me an autographed picture of you.

I own GEORGE WASHING Machine. My Uncle Mooey is depressed because my homemade washing machine wrinkled his shorty pajamas. Every other stripe came off.

Thank you. Please make your picture out to Henry Hamburger Nancy & Victor.

Henry Hamburger Nancy
& Victor (Presidential looking Baboon)

→ Victor
My monkey
who looks like you

You

OMG

My head was spinning. I think it was my head. It could have been a top. But something was spinning. I was related to people who knew presidents and pirates, and even the guy who invented the sandwich. Every time I ate some coleslaw now I would think of the impact my family had on this world, thanks to my relative the Earl of Sidedish. (My father told me about him once when he asked for sliced tomatoes instead of French fries.)

I was sitting in my apartment caring for Loretta Float. She was the one who had bought a lottery ticket at the Shop 'n' Steal and got hit by lightning. It wasn't even raining. Loretta was under my care in a huge paperwork snafu. Somehow wrong papers were filled out and she was my responsibility. I gave her a marshmallow Peep and let her taste cinnamon on a spoon.

"I like you, Ted," she said.

"I like you, too, Loretta," I answered back, as I had twenty-five more pieces of paper to initial concerning her.

The phone rang. It was my publisher, Mary Anne Numb.

"Your latest letters, Mr. Nancy, are impressive. The comedy club one is so well written and the picture of the president of Iceland is dramatic in his full Iceland finery. It is inspiring to get these heads of state to answer you."

I knew I was writing fine literature. She had no idea the correspondence my family had with dignitaries and luminaries.

"I look forward to seeing more for your latest LETTERS FROM A NUT book. Do you also have emails?"

I told her I did, and we chatted for a few more minutes. We hung up. I peeled a poppy seed and went back to work on the latest batch of correspondence I had:

1413 1/2 Kenneth Rd #193
Glendale, CA 91201
TEDLNANCY1@gmail.com

Information
CBD Books On Tape Co.
140 Summit St.
Peabody, MA 01960   12/16/2009
customer.service

Hello CBD Books On Tape Company,

I was told to contact you from my Jelly 'n Jam club. Do you have
the study course: LEARN TO STUTTER IN ANOTHER LANGUAGE. STUTTER
IN FRENCH!

I stutter in English and now I want to stutter in French. I am
taking a trip to Dijon and need to learn the Language to stutter
with French people. I am looking for the full 78 disc Audio Tape
set.

Also...Do you sell ASSORTED DRY HIGHLIGHTERS?

You have been highly recommended by the Sand Castle Association
and i look forward to purchasing the 92 CD Audio Tape set from
you.

Respectfully,

Ted L. Nancy

P.S. I hope I'm not confusing you with the people who repair
books - I believe they are the TAPE ON BOOKS Co.

ients Reader Web more ▼

Search Mail   Search the Web   Show sea
Create a f

« Back to Inbox   Archive   Report spam   Delete   Move to   Labels   More actio

Re: ORDERING FROM YOU (KMM7264411I15977L0KM)   Inbox   X

CustomerService   hide details 6:44 PM (9 minutes ago)

"TED L. NANCY"
<tedlnancy1@gmail.com>
Wed, Dec 16, 2009 at 6:44 PM
Re: ORDERING FROM YOU
(KMM7264411I15977L0KM)

Thank you for your product inquiry. Unfortunately, CBD does not
currently carry "Learn to Stutter in French". If this is a new item, we
recommend that you continue to check our web site in case it is added to
our inventory in the future. You might also try a search of either
Google, Yahoo or Ask.com for additional sources.

We do carry the Dry Highlighters - I have listed the stock number, title
and price below.

9974   WORDKEEPER DRY HIGHLITER ASSORTMENT $3.99

If you have any questions, please let us know.

Customer Service

Information
ENJAMIN FRANKLIN INSTITUTE
_22 North 20th Street,
Philadelphia, PA 19103   Aug 30, 2010
webteam@www.fi.edu

Dear Benjamin Franklin Institute:

I am looking for your BEN FRANKLIN BATH MATS. The same bath mats
Ben Franklin stepped on when he got out of the shower in 1776.

Will they have the spongy surface? Also do you still carry the
BEN FRANKLIN SOAP CADDY? Thank you.

Ted L. Nancy

RE: Inquiry From www.fistore.com

Reply| from Customer Service The Museum Shops
reply-to customerservice@skyretailpartners.com
to "TED L. NANCY" <tedlnancy1@gmail.com>
date Mon, Aug 30, 2010 at 11:08 AM

Ted, My apologies, but we do not have these items in stock. We only have what
is available on the website. Thank you.

Customer Service
The Franklin Institute Store

CUSTOMER SERVICE
BENJAMIN FRANKLIN INSTTUTE   Aug 30, 2010
customerservice@skyretailpartners.com

Dear Benjamin Franklin Institute:

Hmmm? I was sure you had these very popular BEN FRANKLIN BATH
PRODUCTS

Are we talking about the same Ben Franklin? The one that flew the
kite, with the electricity? and invented the Post Office. That
Ben Franklin?

What about the BEN FRANKLIN SILLY STRAW? Do you have that? That
you can bend into glasses. Like Ben Franklin wore in 1776.

Thank you for your customer service answers. it is most welcome.

Ted L. Nancy

RE: Inquiry From www.fistore.com

Customer Service The Museum Shops
reply-to customerservice@skyretailpartners.com
to "TED L. NANCY" <tedlnancy1@gmail.com>
date Mon, Aug 30, 2010 at 11:49 AM

Do you have item numbers for any of the products? I could look them up by item
number to see if we have them backordered. Thank you.

Customer Service
The Franklin Institute Store

TED L. NANCY
Tedlnancy1@gmail.com

CUSTOMER SERVICE
BENJAMIN FRANKLIN INSTITUTE
customerservice@skyretailpartners.com

Aug 30, 2010

Dear Benjamin Franklin Institute:

Thank you for helping me. I have long admired Ben Franklin.

Is this the same Ben Franklin who wore that triangle hat? Worked
on the Declaration of Independence?. Invented the printer, is on
the half dollar? That Ben Franklin?

Your store is supposed to have the: MENTOS-GEYSER TUBE. Makes a
25 foot soda geyser. Just add Mentos candy, pull the trigger, run
away. Can you use it inside?

Thank you for your customer service . You are a professional in
the mold of Ben Franklin. The man with the buckle shoes. (same
Ben Franklin?)

Ted L. Nancy

RE: In

Customer Service
customerservice@skyretailpartners.com
to "TED L. NANCY" <tedlnancy1@gmail.com>
date Mon, Aug 30, 2010 at 12:37 PM

Yes it is the same Ben Franklin. We have the geyser tube, you can look at it on
ur website item number 499080. The website says it can only be used
outside. Thank you.

Customer Service
The Franklin Institute Store

```
                                        TED L. NANCY
                                        Tedlnancy1@gmail.com


Information
Benjamin Franklin House
36 Craven Street, London WC2N 5NF          Aug 30, 2010
info@BenjaminFranklinHouse.org


Dear Benjamin Franklin's House:
I am desperate now!  That is why I an now writing to you in
London.  At Ben Franklin's house.  Do you sell the BENJAMIN
FRANKLIN BATH MATS and BENJAMIN FRANKLIN SOAP CADDY.  I must have
these!

The same soap Ben Franklin put back in the caddy hanging in his
shower to get clean.  Then stepped onto the bath mat when he got
out of the shower in 1776.  before writing the Declaration Of
Independence.  Spongy surface mat, please.

Also do you carry the BENJAMIN FRANKLIN FINGER PUPPET?  (as I have
heard)   Thank you.


      Ted L. Nancy
```

BENJAMIN FRANKLIN SHOWER STUFF

Reply| from Benjamin Franklin House <info@benjaminfranklinhouse.org>
to" TED L. NANCY" <tedlnancy1@gmail.com>
date Tue, Aug 31, 2010 at 2:50 AM
subject RE: BENJAMIN FRANKLIN SHOWER STUFF

Dear Mr. Nancy,

Thank you for your email. Unfortunately we do not stock the Benjamin Franklin
bath mat or soap caddy. To my knowledge we have never stocked either item.

We do however stock the finger puppet, which you can purchase on our online
shop here http://www.benjaminfranklinhouse.org/site/sections/shop/default.htm

Regards,

Sally

Operations Manager
BENJAMIN FRANKLIN HOUSE
36 Craven Street
London WC2N 5NF

BACK ON MY COMPUTER
(I HAVE A MAC)

I was on YOURFAMILYBELONGSINATREE.COM searching for more of my family tree. After a few hours I had nothing. *Is this it? Is this the end of my search? Can I only get to the beginning of the 1800s and George Washington? Surely I have more. I mean I'm here, aren't I? Someone had to keep the family tree going to get to me,* I thought.

"Ted, can you get some crumbs out of my eyebrows?" It was Loretta Float. "My eyebrows are full of cinnamon crumbs."

"Yes, hang on, Loretta. I'll brush them off in a minute."

Just then I saw an email in my inbox. It was from a name I did not recognize. "Mr. Nancy, my name is Dagmar Toiletseatgaard and I have an old newspaper dated 1844 in my hands with regards to a family member of yours named Edward Allan Nancy. Can we talk?"

We sure can talk, I thought.

I was at the airport for my Jet Blue Flight #201B to Denmark. What I like about Jet Blue is that the name of the airline sounds like a urinal cake. I was seated in business class. What I like about business class is the people in coach hate you and you hate the people in first class, so you have a nice rhythm going on. I settled in for the enjoyable seventy-two-hour flight to Denmark. I was restless after fifteen minutes. SAMMY!

I was at my hotel in Odense, Denmark, the birthplace of Hans Christian Andersen. I only stay at Mongolian hotels and their Rameda Tsagdaa Duudaarai Mongolian Hotel is superb. In English their hotel name translates to "Call the police!"

In the bathroom, I remember that in my *Even More Letters from a Nut* book, written in the mid-nineties, I had taken the paper sanitary toilet-seat guard off the commode, popped out the middle, and made a cowboy hat out of it. Funny, I was now going to see a woman with the last name of Toiletseatgaard. Isn't life interesting? So in honor of her, I punched out the middle of the sanitary toilet-seat guard and put it on my head once again and answered the knock on my door that way. It was room service. Within four minutes I was line dancing while the waiter rushed through his food setup. I tipped him seventy-two million dakmenshven (which is three cents) and he left.

After a rest of one hundred and forty-seven hours in my hotel room, I headed out to see the Danish women who had emailed me.

Odense was a fairy-tale village much like the acclaimed author's fairy tales took place in. If you're not familiar with Hans Christian Andersen, he wrote some of the greatest fairy tales in history: *Thumbelina*, *The Little Mermaid*, *The Princess and the Pea*, *The Emperor's New Clothes*. Apparently he also had my relative Edward Allan Nancy on his back his entire career for similar stories, as we shall soon see.

DAGMAR TOILETSEATGAARD was a round-faced woman with short blonde hair. Her eyes were loopy and she had a weird toothy smile. She looked curiously like Hillary Clinton. "I get that a lot," she said. "Especially when I wave to people in motorcades. Won't you come in?"

Dagmar had a little cottage she lived in. She was a hoarder, meaning she collected old newspapers, shoes, dishes, stacks of stuff; she never threw anything away. We had to walk over a lot of junk piled up to find a place to sit and talk. Finally we sat on a pile of trash.

"Mr. Nancy, I want you to see this newspaper I have from the 1800s. It appears to be from an ancestor of yours, Edward Allan Nancy."

I took the newspaper and looked at it.

"I have been reading up on you, being that I like your books. All I read are LETTERS FROM A NUT and assembly instructions for old electronics. It seems you have quite the history, Ted."

I have to admit the newspaper from 1844 was exciting to look at. Edward Allan Nancy had the same last name as me, and as far as I know, all the Nancys were related. And then, like finding a treasure chest, she opened one of the piled-up cartons and pulled out old mail, envelopes, and more newspaper articles and pictures and showed them to me.

"These were left to me by my grandfather Gorscht. Right before he was admitted to Goornersvarg Insane Asylum in Ballerup. That's in the Smorgasbord Hills. Are we related, Mr. Nancy?"

Civilization Flourishes
While My Family
Hits the Wall

1801 – 1900

EDWARD ALLAN NANCY, JR.
1855 – 1933

EDWARD ALLAN NANCY
1811 – 1889

EDWARD ALLAN NANCY: Considered a crackpot, he assumed many identities. Photos found of him had him living as different people.

EDWARD ALLAN NANCY, JR.: His son was also considered unbalanced.

THE MORNING DANISH

COPENHAGEN, DENMARK WEDNESDAY, JANUARY 3, 1844

LUNATIC SUES WRITER

Edward Allan Nancy

Failed fairy tale author Edward Allan Nancy of Baltimore filed suit in Federal Court claiming acclaimed author Hans Christian Andersen has been stealing his works for years. Nancy, who has never been published and has a history of "illness", said today: "His Humpty Dumpty and my Larry Dumpy are the same. His Emperor's New Clothes and my King's Irregular Trousers are just too similar." Nancy is represented by attorney Marcus Saltshaker known for his ridiculous slip and fall lawsuits.

Hans Christian Andersen

Edward Allan Nancy
21 Usher House
Baltimore, Maryland

Hans Christian Andersen
#17 Prune Danish Rd.,
Odense, Denmark   Feb 5, 1844

Dear Hans Christian Andersen:

I am sorry it has to come to this - me suing you. But you have been "taking" my stories and saying you wrote them. It's obvious your "UGLY DUCKLING" is a direct steal from "MY DUCKLING WITH BAD HAIR". It's the same story! Your Ugly Duckling looks at his reflection in the water, my Hair Plug Duckling has to wear a cheap toupee after putting goo on his head. DON'T YOU SEE THE RESEMBLANCE?! GOOD GRIEF!

Your "LITTLE MERMAID" from 1836 and my "HOTEL MAID" . Puhleeze! Yours is a mermaid willing to give up her life in the sea to gain the love of a human prince. My Hotel Maid is about a cleaning lady who yells "housekeeping" all day . ISN'T THIS THE SAME ?!! A MAID'S A MAID WHETHER SHE'S IN THE SEA OR IN THE ROOM!   Hans, what are you doing? Open a window! It's theft. I try to be fair, I want to be fair. BUT HOW MUCH MORE CAN I TAKE?! (i can take a little more)

Then there's your "PRINCESS AND THE PEA" about a search for a real Princess so they stack 20 mattresses up with a pea under the bottom one to see if she can feel the pea. My story "THE KING AND THE BROCCOLI" is just too close!!!! Hello! Just lie down on a broccoli and see what I mean. Can you not see this? And don't even get me started about Larry Dumpy, Humpty's brother. Sad. You disgust me.

Edward Allan Nancy

Hans Christian Andersen
#17 Prune Danish Rd.
Odense, Denmark   Feb 17 1844

Edward Allan Nancy
21 Usher House
Baltimore, Maryland

Dear Mr. Nancy:

Are you nuts? Vanvitting? I am appalled you would think I take from
your stories.

Next you'll tell me my story THE EMPERORS NEW CLOTHES about a
man who walks around with no clothes on - people realizing he is not
what he appears to be - is the same as your story I just finished
reading: HANSEL AND GRETEL AND LARRY .   (I did not care for
your story; lose Gretel. I do like Larry though. I see him as a man who
uses a handkerchief a lot)

It is you who are vanvitting. Ikke generer mig med dit vrøvl (Do not
bother me with your nonsense)

I am appalled! Go away! Gornscmins

Hans C. Andersen

Edward Allan Nancy
21 Usher House
Baltimore, Maryland

CUSTOMER SERVICE
GREAT AMERICAN BAKING TIN COMPANY
17B Crabcake Cove
Baltimore, Maryland   May 5, 1848

A good day to all:

I own EDGAR ALLAN PIE. We sell pies. Some of the finest in all of
Baltimore, I am told.

I need to order tins from you on a daily basis. Our pies are apple,
cherry, Boston Creme, mince. YES WE HAVE SMOKED PIT PENDULUM
CRUSTS! (Must be on each tin.)

Can you assist me.? I need to start immediately with this large order.
WE HAND MAKE RAVEN TARTS! (must be on pie box)

I have cleared this with the famous author Edgar Allan Poe. I do not
believe this confuses the public. He writes books and poems like the
Raven, I sell Raven cupcakes.

He write stories like "The Fall Of The House Of Usher" we are working
out of a house on Usher Blvd. No one fell. There should be no
confusion.

Let us do business and avoid all horror and mystery that sometimes
comes from pie and book confusion.

Thank you, I remain....
Edward Allan Nancy
Owner Edgar Allan Pie (formerly Conquerer Worm Farm)

LAW FIRM OF MORRIS, MORRIS, MORRIS AND NOT MORRIS

217 Oyster Way
Baltimore MD

Edward Allan Nancy
21 Usher House
Baltimore, Maryland   May 20, 1848

Re: CEASE AND DESIST

Dear Mr. Nancy:

Your letter has been turned over to this law firm by the Great American Baking Tin Co.

This firm represents Edgar Allan Poe, the acclaimed author. It has come to our attention that you are attempting to use Mr. Poe's valuable good name to confuse the public with your EDGAR ALLEN PIE business.

This is to inform you that you are to Cease and Desist immediately. Mr. Poe in no uncertain terms wants his works confused with pies, cupcakes, tarts, crusts, tins, or anything involving baked goods.

We hope this letter acts as Mr. Poe's desires on this matter. And we assume no further legal action is required. However we will be vigorous if needed

Good day, Sir

Mordecai Thaddeus Zebulon
Not Morris
Law Firm of Morris, Morris, Morris, & Not Morris

Edward Allan Nancy
21 Usher House
Baltimore, Maryland

PHINEAS T. BARNUM
124 E 10th St.
New York City, New York

July 4 1855

My Dear Mr. PT Barnum.

May I introduce myself? I believe you already know my famous brother, TOM THUMB. I am LEE THUMB. Tom Thumb is your star attraction. He is a 2 foot 1 inch, 53 pound tiny man. people all over the world look at him as he does nothing. He's General Tom Thumb! I AM ADMIRAL LEE THUMB. I am of normal height, 5 feet 10 inches, 170 pounds. I also do nothing. Let's put me in the show! (My legal name is Edward Allan Nancy)

In my talks with Mr. Thumb, he gets depressed and surly complaining that peoples hold him in their sweaty palms and squeeze him too tight. One belched an avocado on him. What kind of garbage is that? hey, what time is it there in New York ?. It's 3 o'clock here and I just made a fizzy noise. Tom says he is tired of being small. One person called him Fun Size. I HAVE TO LIVE WITH THIS MANIAC!!!

My act consists of darting around, milling about, wondering over there, moving back and forth, barking out fast food orders, yelling out barb que sauces. I do this for 3 hours. But with the LONGER version I do 75 more minutes of moving around, shifting about, wearing a hat, barking out shrimp dinners, wearing a bib. You can bill me as Lee Thumb . His real name is not Tom Thumb. It's Ralph Hem. THIS MAN IS NUTS!

Please consider me for your consideration in considering me for you.

Thank you,
LEE Thumb Nancy
Lee Thumb Nancy
Edward Allan Nancy

NO REPLY

84

(Not to scale)

THE THUMB BROS. TOM & LEE

Edward Allan Nancy
21 Usher House
Baltimore, Maryland

Reservations
WILLARD HOTEL
1401 Pennsylvania Avenue NW
Washington, DC 20004   Apr 1, 1865

Dear WILLARD HOTEL Reservations.

The goodest of mornings! So nice to communicate with a residence such as yours. Very professional and so welcome in this time of Civil War to our great nation. MUSKET! (Pardon me I have a medical condition causing me to yell out battle references).

I will be arriving by canon 11 Apr, 1865 and will need lodging for 3 nights. dusty unpaved road view. Thank you.

I will sit in in your lobby and bark out the name Sherman over and over again to whoever passes. This goes on for 9 hours. Will it bother staff? many delicate ladies do not like to be yelled at as Sherman. PLEASE, LAST TIME YOU PUT MY BY THE ICE MACHINE!! THE NOISE KEPT ME AWAKE.

The last time I stayed in your hotel I must tell you I went down to the restaurant and was agitated. I normally eat at a favorite spot in your restaurant and to my discomfort I asked for the same place and was told: "I am sorry that's John Wilke's booth." The nerve of John Wilkes. Do you still serve mutton chop melts.?

Can you get me tickets to Ford's Theater for Apr 14, 1865. To see Elias Dunham and his puppet Peanut? Who's funnier then Elias Dunham? (and his purple puppet)   I look forward to a relaxing stay.

With Utter Respect,

Edward Allan Nancy

THE WILLARD
"WASHINGTON'S FINEST HOTEL
TO SIT IN THE LOBBY AND YELL THINGS OUT"

RESERVATIONS
WILLARD HOTEL
1401 PENNSYLVANIA AVENUE NW
WASHINGTON, DC 20004   APR 6, 1865

EDWARD ALLAN NANCY
21 USHER HOUSE
BALTIMORE, MARYLAND

DEAR MR. NANCY:

WE CAN OFFER YOU OUR STOVEPIPE HAT ROOM FOR THE NIGHTS OF
APR 11 THROUGH APR 13. YOU WILL HAVE NO ROOM FOR THE NIGHT
OF APR 14 AS YOU REQUESTED ONLY 3 NIGHTS LODGING. THAT IS
THE NIGHT YOU WANTED FOR THE PLAY WITH ELIAS DUNHAM. AND WE
AGREE, WHO'S FUNNIER THAN ELIAS DUNHAM? (HE HAS NOW ADDED
HIS CONFEDERATE COLONEL JALAPENO ON A STICK TO HIS ACT.)

HOWEVER WE EXPECT PRESIDENT LINCOLN TO ATTEND THE THEATER
THAT NIGHT OF APRIL 14, 1865 TO SEE HIS FAVORITE PLAY:
"ELIAS DUNHAM & PEANUT - PLEASE USE SOME MOUTHWASH!"
SO WE CANNOT MAKE RESERV. FOR YOU.

HOWEVER, YOUR STAY INCLUDES A FREE GETTYSBURGER IN OUR
RESTAURANT. THANK YOU FOR CHOOSING THE WILLARD.

SINCERELY,

Molly O'Boy

MOLLY O'BOY
RESERVATIONS ATTENDANT

EDWARD ALLAN NANCY JR.
12 Rumpskeen St
Crumple, Massachusetts

To: Thomas Edison
127 Gormish Dr. Menlo Park, NJ   Dec 5, 1880

Dear Mr. Thomas A. Edison.

Let me say hello to you, my fellow inventor. Hello. I am an inventor too. I know you invented the lightbulb, the phonograph, and the haircut. Impressive. Would you please consider my invention: THE YUMBRELLA.

This is an umbrella you use when it rains and. when it stops raining you eat it. no need to have it drip in your foyer (see illustration encl.)

Hey! (That's all i got)

I know you say. "Genius is 1 percent inspiration, 99 percent perspiration." Wonderful saying! Marvelous! How about inventing something for those that perspire 99 percent of the time. Please consider my YUMBRELLA. I can only get so many messages out from where I am. BTW: You can eat your umbrella in 2 minutes. Also comes in Chipolte . Thank you, Mr. E.

Edw all— Nang Jr.
Edward Allan Nancy Jr.

Thomas Alva Edison

Edw. Allan Nancy Jr.
12 Rumpskeen St., Crumple, Mass.   Jan 1 4, 1881

Dear Edw. Allan Nancy Jr.

Thank you for noticing my perspiration quote.   It came to me effortlessly.
Regarding your Yumbrella.   I must tell you we have a similar idea here at our
Menlo Park Laboratory.   Ours is called: CHEWLACE.   You eat your
shoelace after you tie your shoe.

You have a fertile mind and one day I expect to see the name Edward Allan
Nancy Jr. involved in greatness.

Sincerely,

Thomas A Edison

EDWARD ALLAN NANCY JR.
12 Rumpskeen St
Crumple, Massachusetts

HENRY HEINZ
   HEINZ KETCHUP COMPANY
      1 Main St.
Pittsburgh Pennsylvania   May 2, 1888

My Dear Good Mr. Henry Heinz.

I am now aware YOU invented Ketchup. Splendid. A need for
this. I was looking for a reddish thick sauce I could put on my
burger when I stumbled upon your Heinz Ketchup. However it
is messy and much waste as NO ONE eats all the ketchup they
pour.

I was pondering, what about: KETCHUP CHEWS. Simply unwrap
a Ketchup Chew and pop it in your mouth. Eat your burger,
keep a Ketchup Chew in your mouth between your cheek &
gums. No messy bottles, no messy spills, just chew. My
neighbor's name is Heinz.

Sincerely,
Edw. All~ Nncy Jr
Edward Allan Nancy Jr.

HEINZ KETCHUP CO.

2 Varirities

1 Main St.
Pittsburgh Pennsylvania

EDWARD ALLAN NANCY JR.
12 Rumpskeen St
Crumple, Massachusetts   Aug 12, 1888

Mr. Nancy Jr.

Thank you writing with your idea for a Ketchup Chew.

At this time we would not consider such an idea.

However, I would encourage you to consider other items to submit to the Heinz Ketchup Company in that we are always on the lookout for bright idea men as yourself.

Respectfully.

Henry Heinz

Edward Allan Nancy Jr.
12 Rumpskeen St
Crumple, Massachusetts

The Eiffel Tower
Monsieur Alexandre Gustave Eiffel
1 Champ de Mars Paris, France   Oct 28, 1889

Dear Monsieur Alexandre Gustave Eiffel,

In a world where everyone complains, I want to NOT complain and single out the employees of your Eiffel Tower in Paris. I visited the Tower a week ago. (I am from Belgium & enjoy tight socks) And your gift shoppe employees, one was named Gigi, helped me out in a BIG way.

I became stuck in the toilet in the mens room in the Eiffel Tower. I was really squished in there. My head, legs, torso, sandal, everything was stuck. I don't know how I even got inside the toilet. I believe i was disoriented from eating expired Marshmallow Peeps.

The fine folks at the Eiffel Tower Gift Shop finally heard the repeated flushing and helped me up and out. They really worked on me for 9 hours with a shoe horn. Only after yelling in Dutch: "IK ben in de stinkende vastgeklemd" which luckily Gigi knew as: "I am wedged inside the Smelly."

Please thank the entire Gift Shop for me. Although Gigi had a disgusting freckle with a hair on it that brushed against my face repeatedly. I called her Roy once in my disorientation.

The Eiffel Tower is a tower that really cares about their visitors and not so much about their dented and ruined shoe horn. I bought a coconut head in the Gift Shop after I was freed! I named it Roy. Please write me and let me know that they were thanked.

Sincerely,
Edward Allan Nancy Jr.

↑
coconut head
I bought

EIFFEL TOWER CONCIERGE
CLAIRE DU MONGE
1 CHAMP DE MARS, PARIS, FRANCE

MONSIEUR EDWARD ALLAN NANCY JR.
12 RUMPSKEEN ST
CRUMPLE, MASSACHUSETTS   NOV 15, 1889

BONJOUR MONSIEUR LE NANCY:

I AM CLAIRE DU MONGE, ASSISTANT TO MONSIEUR EIFFEL, AND YOUR
LETTER HAS BEEN NOTED.

WE HAVE THANKED THE ENTIRE STAFF OF OUR GIFT SHOPPE. THEY DO
REMEMBER THE INCIDENT AND ARE GLAD YOU ARE DOING FINE. GIGI IS NO
LONGER WITH US. SHE HAS LEFT OUR EMPLOY TO WORK AT THE STATUE
OF LIBERTY IN NEW YORK.

YOU'LL BE HAPPY TO KNOW THAT BECAUSE OF YOUR INCIDENT IN LE
COMMODE , WE HAVE MOVED THE MENS ROOM FROM THE TOP OF THE
EIFFEL TOWER TO THE MIDDLE, MAKING IT CLOSER TO THE GIFT SHOPPE
SO SCREAMS CAN BE HEARD MORE EASILY.

IN ADDITION, WE ALSO THANK YOU FOR PURCHASING A COCONUT HEAD
FROM THE SHOPPE. IT IS ONE OUR MORE POPULAR ITEMS ALONG WITH
CHATTERING TEETH.

MERCI BEAUCOUP,

CLAIRE DU MONGE FOR
MONSIEUR GUSTAVE EIFFEL

Edward Allan Nancy Jr.
12 Rumpskeen St, Crumple, Massachusetts

STATUE OF LIBERTY
Liberty Island , New York, NY 1   4 July, 1890

Dear Customer Service, Statue Of Liberty.

In a world where many complain of others - i would like to
NOT complain of others but instead PRAISE an employee of your
Statue Of Liberty. Recently I visited your Statue when I became
confused. I believe it was from eating tainted mule. I got stuck
inside your lint vent. I was really crunched up in there. My
head, torso, lap, flip flops were all in there. I was stuck for a
good 10 hours. It was not until an employee from your gift
shop heard me yell: "Ik ben squished binnen uw lint
ontluchtingsinrichting en hebben gegeten 5 1/2 bezoedelde mule."
Which is: "I am squished inside your lint vent and have eaten 5
1/2 pounds of tainted mule" in Dutch. I believe her name was
Gigi and she squiggled me out with a chop stick.

She should be commended. A plaque should be given her. I
called her Ralph for 10 minutes straight in my disorientation.
She had a rubbery mole which bounced on me causing nausea.
Please let me know she was thanked. I also bought a **salami
face** from your gift shop.
Edward Allan Nancy Jr

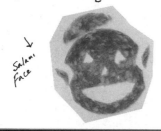

↓
Salami
Face

← Lint vent
where i was
stuck

CUSTOMER SERVICE DEPARTMENT
STATUE OF LIBERTY
LIBERTY ISLAND
NEW YORK, NY 1

EDWARD ALLAN NANCY JR.
12 RUMPSKEEN ST
CRUMPLE, MASSACHUSETTS   15 JULY, 1890

DEAR MR. NANCY:

THANK YOU FOR WRITING TO THE STATUE OF LIBERTY WITH YOUR LINT
VENT PROBLEM. WE ARE SORRY YOU EXPERIENCED A LESS THAN PLEASANT
VISIT. I SPOKE WITH OUR GIFT SHOP AND THEY WERE FAMILIAR WITH THE
INCIDENT. I CONVEYED YOUR APPRECIATION. HOWEVER GIGI IS NO LONGER
WORKING AT THE STATUE OF LIBERTY. SHE IS NOW AT A WATER THEME PARK
IN ORLANDO, FLORIDA.

ADDITIONALLY, WE MOVED THE MENS ROOM FROM LADY LIBERTY'S CROWN
TO HER TORCH. THE LINT VENT WILL NOW BLOW INTO THE SKY. SHOULD
YOU GET STUCK IN THE VENT AGAIN YOU CAN ALWAYS GET OUT THROUGH
THE TORCH.

WE WANT YOU TO KNOW, MR. NANCY, THAT WE LISTEN TO OUR VISITORS.
WE WANT TO MAKE ALL OUR GUESTS COMFORTABLE.

ENCLOSED PLEASE FIND A COUPON FOR A STATUE OF LIBERTY PANCAKE &
SAUSAGE ON A STICK. THANK YOU FOR WRITING US.

SINCERELY,

JANE CHANG
CUSTOMER SERVICE
STATUE OF LIBERTY

50% off

Edward Allan Nancy Jr.
12 Rumpskeen St
Crumple, Massachusetts

MR. AND MRS. ANDREW BORDEN
92 Second Street,
Fall River, Massachusetts   June 15, 1892

My Dear Mr. & Mrs. Andrew Borden.

I am answering your advertisement where you wish to marry
off your lovely daughter, Lizzie Borden. She sounds like a
delight. May I see a picture of her.?

My name is Edward Allan Nancy Jr. and I am of fine stock,
good back, and with all my teeth. One arm is shorter then the
other although I do not know which one. TROMBONE! Excuse
the outburst. I suffer from a rare syndrome. I yell out
musical instruments from the 1890 s. ZITHER!   (i am sorry)

I expect to be in the Fall River, Massachusetts area soon and
would love to also secure lodging at your home while I visit
your Lizzie and we discuss marriage. May I call on her soon?

Respectfully,
Edward Allan Nancy Jr.

MR. AND MRS. ANDREW BORDEN
92 Second Street
Fall River, Massachusetts

Edward Allan Nancy Jr.
12 Rumpskeen St
Crumple, Massachusetts   Aug 1, 1892

Dear, Dear Mr. Nancy Jr.,

What a delight to hear from you. In these slow times of mail delivery your answer to our advertisement was quite speedy.

So nice of you to inquire of our daughter Lizzie Borden. My wife Abby and I, we welcome you to our home.

August 4th would be a most wonderful time for you to stay overnight and visit with Lizzie who is of sound mind, stable thoughts, and has recently had a freckle removed without anesthesia.

We look forward to your visit and stay with us on Aug 4, 1892. It will be a most glorious day.

Please find enclosed a photo of our lovely Lizzie.

Sincerely,

Andrew & Abby Borden

I'M GOING TO FAINT

Who knew all this was going on before me. Huh? Denmark was riveting. I belched up a macaroon and called my father a lint. The Danish peoples were very nice to me. JANNIK! I found new names to yell out, these being Denmark men's names. MEINERT! I met new peoples, ate Denmark foods of herring and corn paste and gornch, which is a hollowed-out rye bread with a happy face on it. I toured the villages, wore a spoirtnz, which is a hat that looks like underwear on your head, saw a DreamWorks panda movie, and found more relatives with the Nancy name. It was apparent that the gene I possessed was given to me by my long line of blood relations. But I was now home, back in my apartment working on my new LETTERS FROM A NUT book.

"Ted, I have a pebble in my shoe. Can you get it out?"

It was Loretta. Loretta Float. And how she got a pebble in her shoe is anyone's guess. Loretta was stiffened out like a piece of driftwood. She was living on my couch because of, as I mentioned, a paper-work mess.

"Hang on a second, Loretta. I'm just assembling some new material for my book." I started calling myself Fred. Just to mix it up.

"Can you face me away from the back of the couch? Pleaeeeese. The little chenille-ball fringes are right near my nostril. It's lightly brushing against my nose. The wispiness bothers me."

"Give me a minute. I'll move you around," I said.

I got a text on my cell phone: "Ted, hoping to see more letters. When? Mary Anne Numb, your publisher."

I looked at the letters and emails and replies I had. I must say I thought they were very good. And I was on the same track as my ancestors.

TED L. NANCY
1413 1/2 Kenneth Rd. #193
Glendale, CA 91201

Information
CHAMBER OF COMMERCE GERMANY
IHK Service-Center
Schillerstraße 11
60313 Frankfurt am Main, GERMANY   Jul 30, 2010

Dear German Chamber Of Commerce

I am seeking assistance. I will be putting on the show:

SNOW WHITE AND DWARFS 8 THROUGH 14

This is a telling of the famous fairy tale after Snow White & The
7 Dwarfs. In that original Sleepy, Sneezy, Dopey, Grumpy, Happy,
Bashful, & Doc ended up running an eyeglass store in the mall.
My story picks up after that and we follow: Jumpy, Fudgy, Creepy,
Lazy, Hottie, Tuna Roll, & Gil The Paramedic .

This will be in Germany for a 16 month run. I need a list of your
Theaters in Berlin so i may stage my play. Germany is a wonderful
theater town.

I once saw "Auntie Mame" there. Carol Channing fell from her
suspended wire. She dragged her foot the entire show. (Think it
was her) Your citizens appreciate good quality and dignified art.
Of which i present.

I once saw "Oklahoma" in Germany. Gordon MacRae fell into the
Orchestra Pit. He wore a knee brace the rest of the performance
and limped towards his sweetie. (think it was him)

May use Betty White instead of Snow White. This is under the
direction of Fabreze Wilson. Let her soak her socks out in the
snack room coffee pot before contacting her.

Thank you for your assistance,

Ted L. Nancy
Ted L. Nancy

Industrie- und Handelskammer
Frankfurt am Main

ndustrie- und Handelskammer Frankfurt am Main, 60284 Frankfurt

Mr. Ted L. Nancy
1413 1/2 Kenneth Rd. # 193
Glendale, CA 91201
USA

Ihr Zeichen, Ihre Nachricht vom	Unser Zeichen, unsere Nachricht vom ISC/HM	Telefon 069 2197-1280	Frankfurt am Main 03.08.2010

Dear Mr. Nancy:

Thank you for your letter dated July 30, 2010.

The Chambers of Commerce are the first port of call for all business matters. Theaters are cultural entities and therefore not our members.

The addresses of theatres in Berlin can be located easily on the internet. In my opinion, the following theatres might be interested in the promising project outlined in your letter:

Theater des Westens www.stage-entertainment.de
Berliner Ensemble Gesellschaft www.berliner-ensemble.de
Friedrichstadtpalast www.friedrichstadtpalast.de

We wish you best results in your endeavours.

Kind regards

Frankfurt Chamber of
Commercen and Industry
Service-Center

1413 1/2 Kenneth Rd. #193
Glendale, CA 91201

Customer Service
HEINZ KETCHUP
P.O. Box 57,
Pittsburgh, Pennsylvania, 15230   Nov 21, 2009

Dear Heinz Ketchups,

I am a long time eater of your ketchup. i yum it up. To me Heinz
is the finest ketchup out there. But now I am confused.

I bought a package of HEINZ KETCHUP SLICES yesterday. I did not
know you made this. Is this you? Here is what it says on the
package:

"KETCHUP SLICES. "No more spills and messes with ketchup the old
fashioned way. With Ketchup Slices you get an individual slice of
ketchup to put on your sandwich so you have an even bite of
ketchup in every mouthful. No more 1 gob of ketchup in 1 bite and
no ketchup in another bite. No messy bottles! No messy spills,
just peel and place."   (which i did)

While this is a good idea - a slice of ketchup so you get an even
mouthful each time - it then said on the same package:

"And now Ketchup Slices comes in new Liquid Form. Just tap the
bottle and pour out a nice dollop of ketchup on your food. No
more slice of ketchup".

The ketchup slice looks like it was one of those knockoff brands
like they have with the fake purses with pictures of Miley Cyrus
on them so i am afraid to eat it.

What should i do, Heinz? Thank you for being a fine company that
answers their customers questions. (my neighbor's name is Heinz)
Call me Fred. I need that.

Sincerely,

Fred D. Nancy
Fred D. Nancy

Heinz North America

Consumer Resource Center

Division of H.J. Heinz Company, L.P.

Heinz 57 Center
357 6th Avenue
Pittsburgh, Pennsylvania 15222-2530

Phone: 1 800 255 5750
FAX: 1 412 237 5291

November 25, 2009

Dear Mr. Nancy:

Thank you for your letter about Heinz Products.

While we wish we could be of help, ketchup slices is not our product.
Please refer to the product packaging for further information about
the manufacturer, or contact your store for more information.

We regret we were unable to help in this instance. As a way of
thanking you for your interest, we have enclosed a complimentary
coupon for Heinz Ketchup.

Consumer Resource Center

ANNIEY/MROSSI
Enclosure

PS - Introducing Ore-Ida® Steam n' Mash potatoes. Finally, homemade
mashed potatoes are easy enough to make everyday. That's because we
use 100% real potatoes that are already scrubbed, peeled, and chopped
for you. They go from the freezer to the table in less than 15
minutes!   (Visit our website at: http://www.steamnmash.com)

And don't forget the Heinz Gravy!

Mailing Address: P.O. Box 57 Pittsburgh, Pennsylvania 15230-0057

1413 1/2 Kenneth Rd. #193
Glendale, CA 91201

Customer Service
HEINZ KETCHUP
P.O. Box 57,
Pittsburgh, Pennsylvania, 15230   Dec 7, 2009

Dear Heinz Ketchups,

Thank you for answering me on my KETCHUP SLICE question. I am a
long time eater of your ketchup. To me Heinz is the finest
ketchup out there. i yum it up. And thank you for calling me
Fred. I needed that. But now I am even more confused.

I shop at a small market. I see they have a new product called:
HEINZ KETCHUP BLANKETS. I did not know you made this. Is this
you? Here is what it says on the package:

"KETCHUP BLANKETS. No more spills and messes with ketchup the old
fashioned way. With Ketchup Blankets you simply get your burger,
get under your ketchup blanket, eat as much as you want. YOU
control the amount of ketchup in each bite. Ketchup soaks into
you. Can be folded".

This does not seem like you. The blanket look like it was one of
those knockoff brands of the fake car seat covers with a picture
of Lady Gaga on them so i am afraid to eat it.

What should i do, Heinz? Thank you for being a fine company that
answers their customers questions. (my neighbor's name is Heinz;
he was recently removed from the neighborhood).

Sincerely,

Fred D. Nancy

Fred D. Nancy

Heinz North America

Consumer Resource Center

Division of H.J. Heinz Company, L.P.

Heinz 57 Center
357 6th Avenue
Pittsburgh, Pennsylvania 15222-2530

Phone: 1 800 255 5750
FAX: 1 412 237 5291

December 11, 2009

Mr. Fred D. Nancy
193
1413 1/2 W Kenneth Rd
Glendale CA 91201-1478

Dear Mr. Nancy:

Thank you for your letter about Heinz Products.

While we wish we could be of help, Ketchup Blanket is not our product.
Please refer to the product packaging for further information about
the manufacturer, or contact your store for more information.

We regret we were unable to help in this instance. As a way of
thanking you for your interest, we have enclosed a complimentary
coupons for Heinz Ketchup.

Sincerely,

Consumer Resource Center

MROSSI/cl
Enclosure

MANUFACTURER COUPON   Expires 06/10/10

003113955A MRO

50 cents off Heinz Ketchup (Any Size/Any
Variety)

MR FRED D NANCY
193
1413 1/2 W KENNETH RD
GLENDALE CA 91201-1478

RETAIL VALUE $

72429

5 13000 20050 4 (8100)0 72429

Mailing Address: P.O. Box 57 Pittsburgh, Pennsylvania 15230-0057

1413 1/2 Kenneth Rd. #193
Glendale, CA 91201

Customer Service
HEINZ KETCHUP
P.O. Box 57,
Pittsburgh, Pennsylvania, 15230   JUL 26, 2010

Dear Heinz Ketchups,

Thank you for answering me on my KETCHUP BLANKET question. I am a
long time eater of your ketchup. I put it on everything.
Including mustard.   Heinz is the finest ketchup out there. But
now I am even totally more confused.

I shop at a small store. And now i see they have a new product
called: HEINZ KETCHUP TENT. Here is what it says on the package:

"KETCHUP TENT. No more spills and messes with ketchup the old
fashioned way. With HEINZ KETCHUP TENT - You just go inside and
live in there for a total ketchup experience. GET AS MUCH KETCHUP
AS YOU NEED!!!"

This does not seem like you. The tent looks like it was one of
those knockoff brands like the fake shoes with a picture of Taylor
Swift on them so i am afraid to go under it.

What should i do, Heinz? Your name and address is on this.

Thank you for being a fine company that answers their customers
questions. (my neighbor Heinz changed his name to Del Monte and
is now living in the Witness Protection Program)

Sincerely,

F. D. Nancy

Heinz North America

Consumer Resource Center

Division of H.J. Heinz Company, L.P.

Heinz 57 Center
357 6th Avenue
Pittsburgh, Pennsylvania 15222-2530

Phone: 1 800 255 5750
FAX: 1 412 237 5291

August 13, 2010

F D Nancy

Dear Valued Consumer:

Thank you for your recent letter regarding Heinz Ketchup.

Because we believe we can be the most help by talking with you, please call our toll-free number, 1 800 255 5750. Our Consumer Resource Representatives are available Monday through Friday, between 8:30 am and 6:00 pm Eastern Time.

We look forward to hearing from you.

Sincerely,

Consumer Resource Center

1413 1/2 Kenneth Rd. #193
Glendale, CA 91201

Customer Service
HEINZ KETCHUP
P.O. Box 57,
Pittsburgh, Pennsylvania, 15230   April 25, 2012

Dear Heinz Ketchups,

Thank you for answering me on my KETCHUP TENT question. I am a
long time eater of your ketchup. It's all i eat. But now I am
really, really, totally, totally confused. That's 2 reallys & 2
totallys.

I shop at a small store. i now see they have a product called:
HEINZ KETCHUP DOME. Here is what it says on the package:

"KETCHUP DOME. Your Entire street is encased in ketchup. Enjoy
the ketchup experience with others. Let the warmth of ketchup
embrace you, Be ketchup. No one can escape. BECAUSE IT'S ALL
KETCHUP! You decide how much ketchup you want. No messy spills
or globs. An Even amount of ketchup in every bite. Take it
through every pore. You are ketchup."

This does not seem like you. The dome looks like it was one of
those knockoff brands like the fake watches that say Rolux. so i
am afraid to install it on my street. It's 3,000 by 2000.

What should i do, Heinz? Your name and address is on this.

Thank you for being a fine company that answers their customers
questions. my neighbor, Del Monte, hid in a chimney once.

Sincerely,

Fred D. Nancy
Fred D. Nancy

NO FURTHER REPLY!

:ormation
Yiwu Kangyi Knitting Factory
www.queenway.cn

Aug 25, 2010

Dear Hat Maker Company:

I need some hats made and fast! It's a priority. These are for my My video: "HAMSTERS OF THE CIVIL WAR".

Some hamsters fought for the South some for the North. They wore the Confederate uniforms, and the Northern uniforms, Sometimes their hats fell off & you couldn't tell.

This is a very moving video. It shows that even though this country was divided in 1862, the hamsters still fought on. Yes!!

I need tiny hats made. Can you make? These would be straw hats. Because hamsters get hot on the head. You have been highly recommended in the Tiny Hat industry. what is next for us? To make these straw tiny hamster hats. Can you do? i am ready.

Sincerely,

Ted L. Nancy

Re: [f.d.nancy@lycos.com]NEED TINY HAMSTER HATS
Sent By "Amy qi" <queenwaycn@gmail.com>
On: August 25, 2010 7:42 PM

Dear Ted L. Nancy,

Thanks for your inquiry. We can do straw hats as customer's requests. But now,I have some questions as follows:

1) what's the size for the Tiny hamster hats?
2) how to wear the hat on the hamster head, the hamster is so small. maybe the hats would add a clip or string? would you please send the design drawing for us?
3) how many quantities do you want?

These are very important information, when i get your reply, i would send the details to you for your reference. We are looking forward your further information.
Best regards

Amy Qi Yiwu kangyi knitting factory(QueenWay)

I CAN'T TAKE IT!

Who am I related to? Unbelievable. These people write to Tom Thumb. How insane is that? My travels had taken me to Scotland, Germany, and Denmark. I had uncovered relatives I could not believe I had. Now I was contacted by a Vincente del Pinchy, a Venezuelan. He first tweeted me:

"Mr. Nancy, you don't know me. Am stranger. But have info on ur family history. Tweet me back. Vincente del Pinchy."

I knew nothing about Vincente del Pinchy except what I looked up online: that he was interested in lineage and had drapes for sale.

"Ted?"

I heard that familiar voice again.

"Ted, can you help me? I got my feet glued inside two oven mitts. I can't get them off. Puleeezeee!"

How I was stuck with this Loretta person, I will never know.

I made arrangements for her to be cared for and headed for the airport. The traffic was really bad on the freeway. We were going sideways.

Finally, I was on the plane. After ninety-one hours we finally were cleared for takeoff to Venezuela. Two hours into the flight, the pilot parachuted out of the plane.

I was now in Venezuela and rented a car. It was a Ford Freckle, Ford's small, tiny discolored brownish car with a weird hair in it. I got on the freeway in Venezuela. The traffic was even worse than it was in Los Angeles. We were upside down. I thought, *This is some really bad traffic. I better get off at the next exit and try to right myself up.*

I got to my hotel and settled in. My room was horrible. It was dirty. I saw a cockroach throw itself in front of a maid's cart and try to end it all. I was tired and quickly fell asleep. I slept like a baby. I dribbled all over myself and crayoned on the walls. A few hours later I was at my destination:

VINCENTE DEL PINCHY: He opened his door and he had a leaf on his head. "It is hot. That is why I wear a large leaf. It only gets in the way when I pull my T-shirt on," he told me.

And with that, he invited me in and showed me a larger leaf folded over. He unwrapped that leaf, and inside was what was now becoming familiar to me: mail.

I browsed through the contents. Letters, pictures, drawings. They were dated from 1901 to 1959.

"You may keep them, Ted."

"What can I do for you, Vincente?"

"Nothing. All I ask is that you water my head."

And I stood there for a good forty-five minutes with a hose on Vincente's head, watering his leaf.

When I finished, he smiled that teethy smile of his and bid me farewell.

I present to you what Vincente del Pinchy showed me that day:

The World Moves Forward

The Nancys Contribute Nothing

1900 – 1959

FUNYUN T. NANCY II
1920 – 2008

ULYSSES S. NANCY
1878 – 1949

FUNYUN T. NANCY
1863 – 1955

ULYSSES S. NANCY: Son of Edward Allan Nancy, Jr. Many believed he was a Hawaiian princess rather than the man he masqueraded as. Like his father and grandfather, he lived his life as many people.

FUNYUN T. NANCY: Was Ulysses's half brother. The resemblance between him and the photo of Ulysses as a Hawaiian princess is striking.

```
                              Ulysses S. Nancy
                            127 2/3 Place Dr
                            Kitty Hawk, NC


GERONIMO
 123 Scalp Itch Lane
Fort Mayberry , Oklahoma            6/ 10, 1901



DEAR GERONIMO

I am a big fan of yours.  Someone told me your real
name is Gene Gassy.  I once knew an Indian whoSe
name was Chief Jiggly Leg. (he walked funny)  They
lived near my house.  His son was named Phil
Gelfand.  He was in the wholesale moccasin business
and eventually fitted Chief Jiggly Leg with a
corrective moccasin.  They were both nuts.  I heard
Geronimo means "One who yawns".  Let me know.

HeY!  I was wondering, is it OK when I jump in the
pool if I hold my nose and yell out your name?  Huh?
Or when I parachute from a plane I'd like to yell
GERONIMO!!  If that is not OK I'll yell GASSY!!!

Please send me an autographed picture.  I will put
it next to my pictures of Buffalo Boil & Wild Bill
Hiccups.


Respectfully,

Ulysses S. Nancy
Ulysses S. Nancy
```

Best,
GERONIMO

```
                                    Ulysses S. Nancy
                                   127 2/3 Place Dr
                                   Kitty Hawk, NC



Pablo Picasso
17B Funnyface Ln
Madrid, Spain                        10.21 . 1901




Dear Pablo Picasso.

I am your cousin, Steve Picasso. (That is my real
name but most know me as Ulysses Nancy.)  Your
father and me are twins.  He has a weird earlobe,
not me. He asked me to write you and give you some
career direction.  They say you are struggling as an
artist and this art thing is not working out for
you.

Maybe i can help you get a job.  I work for the
Police Department as a sketch artist.  There is a
good living in drawing criminals.  It is steady work
as there is always crime.  Would you consider
drawing criminals as a career in the Police
Department.?  You must have some ability as an
artist if you are trying it.

Enclosed is a picture of me and some of my police
sketch work.  Let me know, Pablo, and I will make
the introduction for you.  Forget this art thing.
Few succeed.  I recently got my neighbor Henri
Matisse a job as a detective.  Believe me I know how
to get the best out of people.


Your Uncle.
```

Ulysses S. Nancy (Steve Picasso)

```
Steve Picasso
(Really Ulysses S. Nancy)
```

NO REPLY

Ulysses S. Nancy
127 2/3 Place Dr
Kitty Hawk, NC

WILBUR & ORVILLE WRIGHT
127 1/2 Place DR.
Kittyhawk, NC   12.11 . 1903

Dear Wilbur and Orville Wright,

So nice to communicate with running down the dirt
road peoples as yourselves. I am your neighbor.
You live at 127 1/2 Place Dr. I live across the
street at 127 2/3 Place Dr. I have the curtains
that say "Help Me".

I once got a catalogue that was supposed to be
delivered to you. They were selling propellers. I
didn't think you needed it. so i threw it away.

I have noticed that you have been trying to get your
FLYING CONTRAPTION off the ground. I must say it is
pretty interesting to see you flop around in this
thing. Sometimes it gets going then crashes,
sometimes it gets an inch off the ground then
crashes, other times theres a long line of people
where you have a security check and they have to
take off their shoes and open their bags BEFORE they
even get on your Flying Contraption. .

I am the guy who sells bags of peanuts on the side
of the road. Would you consider putting peanuts on
your plane? (ahh, its probably a bad idea, forget
it)

feel free to stop buy for a sponge bath for a
nickel. If you look across the street now I am
waving.

Ullyses S. Nancy
Ulysses S. Nancy

WILBUR & ORVILLE WRIGHT
127 1/2 Place DR,. Kittyhawk, NC

Dear Mr. Nancy.

Yes, we are quite aware of you, Wilbur and myself. We ask you stop pestering us with your ideas. Who would eats peanuts on a plane my good gent? Why don't you just suggest people bring all their underwear to the airport! Preposterous.

Orville Wright

Orville Wright
12,28 , 1903

THE UNION PRESS COURIER OBSERVER TRIBUNE GAZETTE AND NEWS

THURSDAY   "ALL THE NEWS WE KNEW"   **DECEMBER 17, 1903**

CRIMINAL CAUGHT FROM POLICE SKETCH

Scoundrel identified through police artist Steve Picasso's sketch.

Phillipe Leotard was taken into custody today after a string of pet shop robberies in Mid City. He was identified through a police sketch drawn by Officer Steve Picasso. "Without Officer Picasso's accurate drawing of the thief, we would not have been able to identify him," says Chief Ernest Tummy.

GAS UP TO A NICKEL A GALLON PUBLIC OUTRAGED!

Gasoline prices zoomed to an all-time high this week. "I won't pay it," says Warren Omelet. "I'll use a horse."

HERSHEY CANDY COMPANY
Main St.
HERSHEY, PENNSYLVANIA   JAN 2, 1928

Dear Hershey Candy Co.

I have been eating your chocolate candy bar for some time now. I was wondering? Why not put your chocolate over some peanut butter?

I was just talking about this yesterday with my neighbors. They are twins. Both work as policemen. Their names are Roy & Ron Reese. They both work at a peanut butter factory here in our home town as security guards.

We call them the REESES PEANUT BUTTER COPS.

Anyway, just a thought - this putting chocolate and peanut butter together type candy invented by my neighbors. (The Reeses Peanut Butter Cops.)

Let me know. Maybe it will catch on.

Sincerely,

Funyun T. Nancy

FROM: Joy Almond Reese
16ll Skittle Lane
Upper Darby, Pennsylvania

TO: Funyun T. Nancy
2107 Nimsy Rd.
Upper Darby, Pennsylvania.

January 29, 1928

Dear Funyun T. Nancy.

I accidentally got your mail delivered to me. It was supposed to go to the Hershey Candy Company but it went to Me, Joy Almond Reese. My father is Roy Reese and he is a cop at the Peanut Butter Factory here in town. You must have sent it to the factory where he works and i got it. I am returning it to you. I am also sending you back the picture you sent. My dad is on the left. Are you the same Funyun T. Nancy that got swallowed in a sinkhole a few years ago?

Joy Almond Reese

FUNYUN T. NANCY II
2107 Nimsy Rd.
Upper Darby, Pa.

Administration
SOUTH DAKOTA STATE OFFICES
1 Main St, Pierre So Dakota   Aug 3, 1947

Dear South Dakota Government Offices:

My name is Funyun T. Nancy II. My father, Funyun T. Nancy, told me
that South Dakota and North Dakota will be changing places. And
that everybody will have to pack their things up and move. Why?
Won't there be confusion? PEOPLE HAVE STUFF! THERE'S NOT
ENOUGH BOXES!!

I like both North and South Dakota where they are and see no need for
this move. Who thought of this? THERE'S NOT ENOUGH NEWSPAPER
TO WRAP GLASSES IF EVERYBODY IS MOVING AT ONCE!

North Carolina and South Carolina are staying where they're at.
(after i wrote them)   West Virginia is moving to the other side of
Virginia to become East Virginia. (at my suggestion) Talk to me after
discussing this move and deciding against it.

What will happen to Mount Rushmore? How can you move all those
faces to another mountain.? THEY WILL CRUMBLE!!. (Practice first
with 100 foot cupcakes. see what i mean) THEY FALL APART! IT WILL
BE A MESS! You'll have half fallen crumbled up faces in the wrong
order. Listen to me. Please. I look forward to my reply.

Funyun T. Nancy II

Do not move
This →

FROM: Joy Almond Reese
16ll Skittle Lane
Upper Darby, Pennsylvania

TO: Funyun T. Nancy II
2107 Nimsy Rd.
Upper Darby, Pennsylvania.

Sept 14, 1947

Dear Funyun T. Nancy II.

I accidentally got your mail delivered to me. It was supposed to
go to Mount Rushmore but it went to Me, Joy Almond Reese. I
am returning it to you. I am also sending you back the picture you
sent to Mount Rushmore. My Uncle Ron is on the right. Are you
related to the Funyun T. Nancy that sent me the Reeses Peanut
Butter Cops letter almost 20 years ago (Swallowed in sinkhole?)

Joy Almond Reese

FUNYUN T. NANCY II
2107 Nimsy Rd.
Upper Darby, Pa.

Base Commissary
  SWISS ARMY HEADQUARTERS
Zurich, Switzerland,   Sept. 19, 1948

Dear Swiss Army Commissary.

I have heard that you now make the SWISS ARMY SHOWER CAP.

This is a shower cap that you bring into the shower that haS all the
things the Swiss Army knife has. I need 1,500 please.

If you need a soup spoon in the shower, simply pull the cord and one
hangs down. Say you want to open a can in the shower and eat ravioli,
the Swiss Army Shower Cap has one on it. Wonderful idea! Simply
marvelous! Its time has come.

If you want to open yOur mail in the shower, a letter opener can be
pulled from your head. Even has a toothpick for removing food from
your teeth in the shower. Revolutionary. Impressive. Do you have it in
maroon?

I would like to order many for our Army heRe in Upper Darby,
Pennsylvania of which i am in charge. (formerly Lower Intestine,
Pennsylvania)

Looking forward to my mail from the Swiss Army Shop. I love your
cheese. .

Respectfully,

Funyun T. Nancy II
Commander Upper Darby Army Squadron 17, Barracks 3
LARRY!

Base Commissary SWISS ARMY HEADQUARTERS
Zurich, Switzerland,

FUNYUN T. NANCY II
2107 Nimsy Rd., Upper Darby, Pa.   Oct 1, 1948

Dear Funyun T. Nancy:

Yes, we do carry the SWISS ARMY SHOWER CAP. We have a few left as we are
phasing this out next year. To make room for the SWISS ARMY PILLOW.
 "Sleep On Over 100 Utensils." If you'd like to order, the model number is SWASC
#2442.

Base Commissary
Swiss Army

SWISS ARMY SHOWER CAP - MODEL: SWASC #2442

"Eat Your Soup In The Shower"

FUNYUN T. NANCY II
2107 Nimsy Rd.
Upper Darby, Pa.

Administration
METROPOLITAN MUSEUM OF ART
1000 5th Avenue, NY, NY 10028

Nov 20, 1959

Dear Metropolitan Museum Of Art.

How delightful to correspond with a building such as yours.   Truly a
delight!   Now. Down to. Why I am corresponding with you:

My Giraffe looks like Leonardo Da Vinci.   His name is Gary.   I have
noticed it when I look at Gary when he eats his leaves.   Also my
mailman - who he has bitten - commented when he said "Your giraffe
looks just like Leonardo Da Vinci. "   My mailman also has big brown
spots on him. But not attractive like Gary's.

I know you have an exhibit now of Leonardo Da Vinci's drawings . I
would like to bring my giraffe to your museum and stand by the
drawings so the peoples can see up close what Leonardo really looks
like . All I would need is :

1. Step ladder
2. Giraffe Holder
3. Bus Fair (from Camden - for 2)
4. Giraffe Munch

I am enclosing a picture of my giraffe Gary.   The resemblance is there.
Your Museum is known for it's cultural displays. Gary would add to
your prestige. (Giraffe odor will be gone by Pennsylvania)

I look forward to your reply and inoculation information for Gary.   Do
you still sell wax lips in your gift shop. ?

Sincerely,
Funyun T Nancy II

"Unparalleled Culture"

Administration
METROPOLITAN MUSEUM OF ART
1000 5th Avenue, NY, NY 10028   Dec 16 1959

MR. FUNYUN T. NANCY II
2107 Nimsy Rd., Upper Darby, Pa.

Dear Mr. Nancy II:

We do not see the resemblance between your giraffe and Leonardo
Da Vinci.   We showed it to our Curator who said your giraffe looks like
Lucille Ball   (See encl. pictures you sent us last year.)

We are not presenting any Lucille Ball exhibits at this time and city
ordinances do not allow any animals over 7 feet on the premises.
(Unless for the impaired such as a Seeing Eye Giraffe)

Yes, we sell wax lips in the gift shop. Is this for Gary the giraffe or your
Postman? We have both.

Sincerely,

Museum Staff

Gary

Gary

A Ted L. Nancy Family Tree Truth

DID HENRY HEIMLICH who invented the HEIMLICH MANEUVER have any other maneuvers?

YES! Henry Heimlich had another maneuver before he invented the Heimlich maneuver.

He put a straw in your ear and tried to blow dislodged food out of your throat that way.

That did not work. The food ended up in your nose.

Epilogue

A New Ted Is Born

1960 – PRESENT

Absent When School Photo Was Taken

TED L. NANCY
1973 –

PHYLLIS MURPHY
1955 –

BARRY MARDER NANCY
1954 –

BARRY & PHYLLIS: These are the parents of
Ted L. Nancy

132

My travels told me the letters stopped in 1959. A final reply from the Metropolitan Museum of Art. And then no more. They answered Funyun T. Nancy II. Now, let me just tell you here and now what happened. Funyun T. Nancy II stopped writing. That is what happened. Here and now. Simple as that. He wrote no more. He put his typewriter away, the same typewriter his father used, and he put his paper and stamps away, the same paper his father had used, and he stopped. And that was it. Funyun T. Nancy II wrote no more.

Some asked why he did not write. Others did not ask. The mystery is shrouded during this time. Who was Funyun T. Nancy II? We know he was my grandfather. But who was he? Funyun T. Nancy II eked out a living. He trained Komodo dragons to care for seniors. "Let us come into your home with our lizards to care for your aged loved ones," his business card said. He would bring a Komodo dragon into a senior's home to help them with their meals, bathing, prescriptions, companionship, and senior breath. The dragons had infectious spittle and bacteria-riddled saliva. There were gnaws and nibbles. The business closed after two days. Funyun II was distraught. He had a new wife to support, having married Cloret Drench in 1953.

Cloret worked at Mercedes Buns, the premier bun bakery in her hometown. These were top-of-the-line hot-dog buns. She counted packages of eight day after day. It was always eight, never six or twelve. She counted with her fingers, a pencil, in columns, four times two, eight in a row, any way she could. She was an expert at this, never missing the eight in each package. This may have contributed to her unbalance.

It was not love at first sight. In fact, Cloret thought Funyun was a stump. "He didn't move," she told her mother. "He stood there for twenty-five minutes while leaves fell on him."

They barely paid the bills. They owed many. They were living off of Cloret's hot-dog-bun-counting job. In 1954 Cloret Drench gave birth to Barry.

At the same time, another couple was falling in love. She was a trampoline demonstrator. She jumped up and down for eight hours a day. Day after day jumping up and down. For eight hours. It was never four hours or twelve hours. Just eight. He sold plus-size Batman wear.

"For the heavy man in your life who dresses like Batman," said his card. He went broke in nineteen hours (overestimating fat men who wanted to dress like Batman in the 1950s). They were married. His name was Roland Smudge, hers was Tammy Clamsy.

In 1955 they gave birth to Phyllis. Barry and Phyllis were the future parents of me, Ted L. Nancy.

There were no more letters written for thirty-five years. Nothing. It had stopped cold. At least, that is what I was told. ENRIQUE! Perhaps they did write letters to businesses and dignitaries but never showed them to anyone? Maybe there were love letters from my father to my mother? Nothing has ever surfaced. It certainly is interesting to think there may be Ted L. Nancy family letters never discovered but out there. I would put that mystery up there with why people named John call themselves Jack. Or why is Hank short for Henry? It's that important.

To continue:

Was that it? Was there to be no more Nancy writings; stopped forever in 1959?

NO!

In 1973 my mother, Phyllis, now eighteen, gave birth. My father, Barry, was at her side. They named the boy Ted. Ted L. Nancy. Me.

In 1974 Barry and Phyllis Nancy went to work at Dozyville Sanatorium and worked there for more than thirty-six years. Some say they did not work there. There were rumors. Dozyville Sanatorium was nestled in Crybaby Hills in Middle Tennessee. They never left.

I was told Dad worked there as a robot repair man. But I have my doubts. My mother also counted hot-dog buns AND demonstrated trampolines. Just like his mother AND her mother. (That is a lot of hot-dog buns counted, a lot of trampolining; just sayin'.) I believe the constant counting of eight buns to a package and the jumping up and down eight hours a day made her unwell. I heard she once tried to squish a ninth bun in there but was caught. Pita bread totally confused her.

I went to live with my grandfather Funyun II, a widower. That's what he told me. I had heard later that Funyun II had a Komodo dragon "incident" and was in a coma for five years. And when he woke up he found out his wife had left him. For another man in a coma.

Grandfather wanted nothing but the best for me. He got half that. Nothing.

Then the letters started up again. Unaware of any of this history, one summer day in 1994, I was eating a bag of Fritos. I noticed on the bag it said: "Got any problems? Questions? Write to Fritos." It stayed in my head, this Fritos thing, for a year. I eventually wrote to Fritos. And they answered me. I guess the Nancy gene, dormant and still all these years, was awakening. BOBO! I would put this event up there with everyone in America commenting, "Why are hot-dog buns eight to a package and hot dogs six to a package?" It's that important. NEIL! (Once again, I am sorry, excuse me. I am being treated.) JIMMY!

Since 1995 there have been many LETTERS FROM A NUT books written by Ted L. Nancy. In all that time no one knew who Ted L. Nancy was. There was a mystery going on. Perhaps that is the way it should be.

But I am here to tell you I am real. There is Me. I know. I wrote this.

I continue to care for Loretta Float. I am working on my new book for Mary Anne Numb.

I carry on my family tree.

Sincerely,

Ted L. Nancy

Ted L. Nancy

EPILOGUE

EPILOGUE

I wonder. A lot.

Why were there no more letters written after 1959?

Until I started up again.

Were there secrets my parents had? Did they write letters to companies, and dignitaries, and celebrities, and regular people—and get them answered—yet show no one?

Were there love letters between my parents that went on for thirty years that no one knows about or has seen?

So I wonder. A lot.

Is there a storage unit out there with these letters from my parents?

And will someone find them like I did?

That would be interesting.

The recently discovered letters from Ted L. Nancy's parents.

It is something to wonder about. Isn't it?

Obviously Ted loves
to get mail!

Write to Ted at:

Ted L. Nancy
1413 1/2 Kenneth Rd. #193
Glendale, CA 91201

Or email at:
ted@tedlnancy.com

His website is:

www.tedlnancy.com

Thanks!